MW00415541

WE CAN
END BIBLE POVERTY
NOW

A Bible in every language
- 2033 p. 63 (portion of Scripture)(agreed by many
- 2020 p. 78   mission groups)
- 2025 p. 78
- 2033 p. 78
  - entire N.T.
    - 2000th anniversary of
      Great Commission and
      ascension of Jesus
* - UniScript - pp. 110-11
* - Source View - pp. 115-17
  - Sphere View - p. 116
  - Verb View p. 117
  - Command View p. 117
* - 7 spheres of influence - p. 101
* - A goal for ending Bible poverty on earth - p. 126

WE CAN
END BIBLE
POVERTY
NOW

LOREN CUNNINGHAM
WITH JANICE ROGERS

YWAM Publishing
Seattle, Washington

YWAM Publishing is the publishing ministry of Youth With A Mission (YWAM), an international missionary organization of Christians from many denominations dedicated to presenting Jesus Christ to this generation. To this end, YWAM has focused its efforts in three main areas: (1) training and equipping believers for their part in fulfilling the Great Commission (Matthew 28:19), (2) personal evangelism, and (3) mercy ministry (medical and relief work).

For a free catalog of books and materials, call (425) 771-1153 or (800) 922-2143. Visit us online at www.ywampublishing.com.

Published by YWAM Publishing
a ministry of Youth With A Mission
P.O. Box 55787, Seattle, WA 98155-0787

Library of Congress Cataloging-in-Publication Data

Names: Cunningham, Loren, author.
Title: We can end Bible poverty now : a challenge to spread the word of God globally / Loren Cunningham, with Janice Rogers.
Description: Seattle : YWAM Publishing, 2017. | Includes bibliographical references.
Identifiers: LCCN 2017011911 | ISBN 9781576589915 (pbk.)
Subjects: LCSH: Bible—Publication and distribution. | Evangelistic work.
Classification: LCC BV2369 .C86 2017 | DDC 266—dc23
LC record available at https://lccn.loc.gov/2017011911

First printing 2017

Printed in the United States of America

To Madison, Kenna, and Liam,
Darlene's and my grandchildren,
and to their generation.
May you see the greatest global
spiritual awakening in all of history.

Contents

Acknowledgments

We want to thank all those who contributed content and helped make this book possible: Amanda Palusky, Amy Cook, Captain Ann Ford, Ben Nonoa, Bernie and Sylvia Kay, Brady Manning, Cheryl Weber, Chong Ho Won, Crystal Cook, Darlene Cunningham, Dave Goetter, David Hamilton, Dax Fears, Dilli (surname withheld for security reasons), Giacomo Coghi, Hans Kristian Sandtorp, Izabella Bodini, Jackson and Anneke Ndecheck, Jeff Rogers, Jill Thornton, Jim Rogers, Joakim Magnus, Joel Rogers, Josiah Palusky, Mark Anderson, Morgan Jackson, Nathaniel Baldock, Neil Sauvageau, Noelle McClure, Petr Samoylich, Rheo Loseo, Runar Byberg, Samantha Arredondo, Shannon Baldwin, Stephanie Palusky, Vae Eli, and Youngshin Kim.

We also want to acknowledge dear friends and co-laborers who have encouraged and inspired this vision: Avery Willis, Dr. Bill and Vonette Bright, Billy Graham, Bob Creson, Bob Hoskins, Brother Andrew, Cameron Townsend, Campbell McAlpine, Corrie ten Boom, Darrow Miller, the David Green family, David and Stephanie Palusky, Dick Eastman, Duncan Campbell, Dr. Francis Schaeffer, George Flattery, George Verwer, Gordon Olson, Dr. Jack McAlister, James Featherby, Jerry and Annette Jackson, Colonel Jim Ammerman, Jim and Joy Dawson, Dr. Kenneth Taylor, Dr. Leland Paris, Michael Perreau, Paul Childers, Paul Eshleman, Dr. Ralph Winter, Roy Peterson, Steve Douglass, Dr. Vishal Mangalwadi, and my father and mother, Dr. J.C. and Jewell Cunningham, and my grandfather,

James H. Cunningham, who was known as "The Walking Bible" because he had memorized so much of God's Word.

Most of all we acknowledge and give all glory to Jesus, the Author and the Finisher.

1

Small Question, Big Challenge

I'm living with a sense of great urgency. It's a growing passion that began long ago. When I wake up in the morning, it's before me. When I go to bed at night, it's there. My coworkers and I have already labored to get this going. But now I feel the Lord is pushing us to finish quickly. Other Christian leaders have been tackling this challenge too—some for decades. It's a job for all of us in the body of Christ. For me it started with a simple question.

In 1966 I was driving with a team of young people to Central America. One of the trailers in our convoy had a breakdown, so we stopped in a dusty Mexican town. While a few of our guys looked for a mechanic, the rest of us went to every home in the town, delivering a Gospel of John and a booklet on how to receive Jesus. Another team held two open-air preaching services in the town plaza, one for adults and one for children.

Someone posed a haunting question that day, one that God used as the beginning of a huge challenge.

After our open-air meeting, a woman in a faded red dress came up to me. My Spanish wasn't very good, but I understood her to say, "There's no Bible in my town, and there aren't any in the towns around here. Do you have a Bible in my language?"

I managed to find a Spanish Bible for her. She clutched it to her chest. "*¡Muchísimas gracias, señor!*"

As we drove away, the woman's question lingered in my mind. *Do you have a Bible in my language?* A picture formed before my eyes. It's what the Bible calls a "vision." I saw a truck about the size of a large moving van. A message painted inside a big circle on its side said, "*Solo los deshonestos temen la verdad. Santa Biblia, gratis.*"

I translated it slowly in my mind. "Only the dishonest fear the truth. Free Bibles."

I marveled at the power of those few words. I had never before heard the first sentence, and my Spanish wasn't good enough to imagine it. Then the vision continued. I saw young people standing in the back of the truck putting Bibles into eager hands as fast as possible.

I knew what the vision meant, so we got started on the challenge right away. When we arrived in Mexico City, I went to the local Bible society to see how many copies they had. Then I phoned friends and raised the money in partnership with the Bible society to buy fifty thousand Spanish New Testaments. Our teams distributed them on university campuses in the city. It was a beginning.

Black Rocks on the Moon

The idea of giving the Word of God to everyone started when I was about seven years old. My family lived in El Centro, California, near the Mexican border.

One night I lay in bed with my arms folded behind my head, studying the bright, full moon. What if we went to the moon, I thought, and wrote the best Bible verse on it? We could find big black rocks up there to spell it out—black because they would stand out on the white moon. We could arrange the rocks to form words big enough so that all the people on earth could read: "For God so loved the world, that he gave . . ."

I stopped. The message had to be shorter. We could never find that many rocks. Maybe we should just write, "God is love."

It was a childish fantasy. No one could reach the moon in the 1940s. And my message in rocks wouldn't reach those who spoke a different language or those who couldn't read at all. But I was thinking and imagining.

Just before I turned twenty-one, the Lord gave me a dramatic "mental movie." It wasn't a daydream, and it wasn't a regular dream. I was wide awake. Whether I closed my eyes or opened them, I saw the images. I've described this experience in my first book, *Is That Really You, God?*

As I watched, I saw a living map of the continents of the world. Waves were crashing on all the shorelines. Each surge that followed went farther and farther across the continents until they covered the entire earth. As I watched, the waves became young people from everywhere taking the Word of God to everyone, everywhere.

That vision formed the foundation for a tiny missionary group called Youth With A Mission, or YWAM. Today it is one of the largest missionary movements in the world.

The vision God gave me after meeting the woman in the faded red dress was a follow-up to the mental movie showing waves of young people. Because the waves turned into youth *carrying the Word of God to the entire world.*

Ending Bible poverty is not some leader's crazy plan. God

birthed the idea. Every vision begins with God, but it is carried out by those who listen and obey.

Later I would find more people who were working on this goal.

Even the Hermit

Over the next few years, during the 1960s and 1970s, YWAM workers delivered Bibles, New Testaments, and Gospels of John to various parts of the world.

In the Caribbean we found Miss Armstrong, our "woman of peace" (see Luke 10:6). She opened doors for us in St. Thomas, including the chance to be on television. On camera I said, "We're going to come to every home on this island to give you a free Gospel of John and a booklet on how to know Jesus personally." One man lived like a hermit high up on the mountain. When two YWAM volunteers reached his home, he said, "I heard on TV what you're doing. I figured you'd never get to me. Yet here you are!"

Suphan Buri Province of Thailand is another example. In 1969 our first around-the-world team took Bibles across rice paddies to every home in the province, even to the hundreds of monks living in Buddhist centers. Likewise, in a few states of Mexico—San Luis Potosí, for example—we placed New Testaments in every home in scores of villages and towns.

Our movement has continued to spread Bibles during more than fifty years of ministry. But the vision connected with the woman in the faded red dress was not yet clear.

2

It's God's Idea

Sometimes a word from the Lord tells you what *not* to do.

In the fall of 1982 I was at a pastors' conference at Campus Crusade for Christ (now called Cru) headquarters in San Bernardino, California. Joy Dawson, Jack Hayford, Rick Howard, and I were the speakers. Three hundred pastors had gathered.

While I sat in the conference listening to Rick, I heard a still small voice. *I don't want you to leave the Hawaiian Islands next year.*

Since I travel 150 to 200 days a year, the message struck me as odd. Going into all the world is part of my calling. Staying home for a year would feel like sitting on the bench instead of playing with the team.

I waited for the reason, but none came.

During the next break, Joy darted over. "Loren! God just told me you're not supposed to leave the Hawaiian Islands next year. Did you hear that?"

"Yes, I heard it. And I told God yes."

"Did he say why?"

"No, but I said yes."

Three Golden Opportunities

Soon I got three special invitations. Dr. Billy Graham invited me to speak at Amsterdam '83, an evangelism conference of thousands of leaders.

Then I got a letter from President Reagan. He asked if I would come to the White House. "I want to talk with you. I've invited ten other Christian leaders." The meeting was planned for January 1983.

Next I received a letter from the Vatican asking if I could meet with Pope John Paul II. The private audience would also be in 1983.

Three golden opportunities from three leaders I would have loved to meet. Yet if I accepted, I would be disobeying God.

Years later I met with Dr. Graham in his home on several occasions. I became a member of one of the boards he chaired. But I never received another invitation from President Reagan or Pope John Paul II.

I began to understand why the Lord told me to stay home in 1983 when I got a phone call from my friend Dr. Bill Bright, the founder of Cru. He told me Congress had declared 1983 the "Year of the Bible" and President Reagan signed it into law. Bill asked me to head up the effort in Hawai'i.

I saw this as the chance to take the Bible to every home in the populated islands.

Even the Forbidden Island

We started with research, using the US census for demographics.

We included the primary language spoken in each area in our planning.

Many of our ministry leaders stepped in. Even with the help we received from the Bible societies and other groups, we needed to raise almost $400,000 to pay for the Bibles. One of our YWAM ministries, a Polynesian dance group called Island Breeze, performed at luaus and brought in some of the funds.

Christians of various denominations joined in. I met with more than six hundred pastors and leaders, both Protestant and Catholic, getting their blessing on the special-edition Bibles we produced. The leading rabbi of the islands endorsed our copies of the Old Testament for Jewish homes. We were able to make Bibles available in each of the fifteen mother tongues of the fiftieth state.

Ni'ihau was a special case. Known as the Forbidden Island, its residents must be Hawaiian. Nonresidents are not allowed to come ashore. They've done this to preserve the Hawaiian culture and language. There are less than one hundred Ni'ihauans. So in order to get Bibles to them, we met with representatives who came by boat to a special event on nearby Kaua'i. I was given the opportunity to make a presentation to them. Afterward they returned to their island with Hawaiian Bibles for every person.

Throughout the islands we alerted the public via television, radio, and full-page ads in newspapers. We said we were coming to their home with a free Bible. We included quotes about how much the Bible meant to Presidents George Washington, Abraham Lincoln, and Ronald Reagan. We included stories of changed lives, marriages restored, nations reformed, and the Bible's impact on Hawai'i in the nineteenth century.

About six thousand people went door to door, offering Bibles to every home. A few people refused to receive God's Word, but most were quite receptive.

It took us a year and a half, but we reached our goal. Giving out those Bibles spread the seed of the gospel all over Hawai'i. During the years following 1983, we watched as new congregations sprang up, some growing into megachurches.

It's Coming!

Why are we saying we want to end "Bible poverty"? What is it? Most Christians know about world hunger and poverty. But many who worship in church every Sunday are not aware of the extreme need for Bibles. Today there are between 165 and 180 million people with no portion of the Word of God available in their mother tongue.[1] Furthermore, roughly three billion people have never heard of Jesus.[2]

The Lord prophesied that before the end comes, everyone will know about him and be exposed to his Word. Revelation 7:9 foresees a multitude from every nation, tribe, people, and language wearing white robes, worshiping before the throne of Jesus. Habakkuk 2:14 promises, "For the earth will be filled with the knowledge of the glory of the LORD as the waters cover the sea." The glory of God is first Jesus, then his followers (John 17:1–26). Notice the Word says everyone will *know* about the glory of God. This verse doesn't promise that all will *accept* Christ. But the knowledge of him will be pervasive, covering the continents like giant waves.

Jesus said the gospel will be preached in the whole world, to all *nations*, before his return (Matt. 24:14). The word for "nations" here is a plural Greek word, *ethnē*. It doesn't mean countries recognized by the United Nations. The singular *ethnos* is a group united by kinship, culture, and common traditions. This includes their mother tongue. Most countries have many *ethnē*.

By the Year 2020

I spoke at a Christian conference in Singapore in 2003. As happens sometimes when I preach, the Lord dropped a powerful idea into my mind. I spoke it out to the crowd. "God wants us to offer Scripture in their language to every household by the year 2020."

Was this idea really from God? All you have to do is ask him. If you're willing to obey whatever he tells you to do, he will make it clear to you.

Later in this book I'll explain how the Lord has been moving to help us reach this goal by 2020. YWAM is privileged to be a small piece of the big puzzle.

Much more is involved than arranging black rocks to spell out "God is love" on the moon. We must be fully committed to this task. The Lord is speaking to others, in various parts of the body of Christ, in many parts of the world. The mission is possible. God wants this to happen, and he has chosen to work through us, his people.

We need to listen to the Holy Spirit and enter into God's passionate desire. Everyone on earth needs the Bible in their mother tongue, the language of their heart. Because this is God's idea.

3

Why Should We
End Bible Poverty?

The number one reason we should end Bible poverty is because God told us to do it. Jesus commanded his followers, "Therefore go and <u>make disciples of all nations</u>, baptizing them in the name of the Father and of the Son and of the Holy Spirit, and teaching them to obey everything I have commanded you" (Matt. 28:19–20).

"Pickling" the Nations

The Bible is the most powerful teaching tool we have. In Matthew 28:19 we find the phrase "baptizing them"—baptizing the nations. How can you baptize a nation?

My friend David Hamilton is a Bible scholar in the original languages of the Old and New Testaments. Recently while working on a project, David read through the entire Bible four-teen times in eighteen months.

I asked him to do a word study on "baptisms" in the Bible. He found many kinds—baptism of repentance, baptism of fire, and baptism of the Holy Spirit, to name a few. But one Greek word for "baptism" stood out: *baptizo*. That is the Greek word the author used in Matthew 28:19 where the context is nations (corporate), not individuals.

It's challenging to discern the meaning of a word used in the Bible two thousand years ago. Just think of the words "awesome" and "awful." They used to be synonyms, meaning "respectful fear." Now they're antonyms, one meaning "won-derful" and the other "terrible."

How can we know what the author meant by a particular word in his day, his culture, his region? We need to find that word used in other literature from the same era.

David searched through old documents, looking for the earliest mentions of the Greek words for baptism, *bapto* and *baptizo*. Finally he found the words, but in a far different setting.

A writer from the early third century AD, Athenaeus of Naucratis, quoted Nicander of Colophon, a Greek cook who lived two hundred years before Christ. The cook described how you could pour vinegar and oil over a turnip to make it tasty. Here he used the word *bapto*. But if you soaked it over a period of time in vinegar and spices—*baptizo*—it would be even more delicious.

(*bapto*)   (*baptizo*)

The ancient chef was comparing a salad dressing to a pickle. In both instances flavor was added, but the salad dressing was a superficial covering. The pickled turnip had a complete trans-formation. Plus, the pickle had staying power.

Many modern translators consider *baptizo* and *bapto* as synonyms, therefore missing the intent of the writer in Matthew

28. He is telling us to "pickle" all the nations, soaking them in the Word of God, teaching them to observe everything Jesus taught us. And we're to do it in the name of the Father, Son, and Holy Spirit.

Changing the Way We Think

Evangelism groups have found that if you lead people to the Lord but have no discipleship with Scripture afterward, most will not be living for the Lord a year later. Sometimes no more than 2 percent will still be followers of Christ.[1]

A group of missionaries decided to document whether adding audio Bibles and community "listening groups" would change this problem. They took a powerful visual gospel presentation into five hundred villages in India. They also brought along audio Bibles. Before they left, they found a person in each village willing to host a listening group for new believers.

They left behind listening groups in all five hundred communities. A total of 6,150 people gathered in those groups to listen to God's Word every week. Other missionaries and local workers visited periodically over the next months to provide more discipleship. The 6,150 listeners grew to more than 15,000. Instead of only 2 percent remaining, they had grown more than 240 percent. Response more than doubled. New Christians multiplied, resulting in 350 new churches.

The missionaries' survey showed in black and white that God's Word enables people to live for Christ.

Finally, Changed Lives

The Bible informs our conscience, awakening us to turn from behavior we've thought of as normal. Paul told the Roman

Christians, "Don't copy the behavior and customs of this world, but let God transform you into a new person by *changing the way you think*. Then you will learn to know God's will for you, which is good and pleasing and perfect" (Rom. 12:2 NLT, emphasis added).

Morgan Jackson, the voice and face of Faith Comes By Hearing, said Christians who read or listen to the Bible in their language usually stop doing immoral things. For instance, he told of a man in Guatemala who said he had been a Christian for a long time. But like other men in his church, he still beat his wife, cheated on her, and got drunk every weekend.

When his tribe received the Bible in their tongue, accepted behavior became unacceptable. After a while this man and others in the church stopped their violent, ungodly ways.

Morgan said this story from Guatemala has been repeated in many other parts of the world. Transformed hearts and minds should be enough motivation for us to take the Word to everyone. Yet there are other compelling reasons.

The Bible Transforms Society

Colonel E. H. Ammerman came to pay his respects at my father's funeral in 2003. I first got to know him in the early 1970s. Later, he often taught at our YWAM schools in Switzerland. Colonel Ammerman, or "Jim," was a senior chaplain for the US Army, sharing responsibilities for the spiritual needs of one hundred thousand GIs all over West Germany.

Following my dad's funeral I sat with Jim and his wife, Charlene.

"Loren, you should hear the latest about the Bible distribution we did in 1972!" Jim said.

I listened eagerly. That Bible distribution on the army bases was one of the most powerful examples of God's guidance and provision I'd ever witnessed.

During the 1970s in our Schools of Evangelism in Switzerland we met daily to engage in intercessory prayer. This is different from other kinds of prayer, such as supplication—carrying our personal petitions to the Lord. During intercession, we wait ✳ to hear what God wants us to pray.

One Monday morning we asked the Lord, "What's on your heart? What do you want us to pray for?"

As we waited in silence, someone in the group said, "I think we're supposed to pray for the US military in Germany."

When someone else confirmed that impression, I thought to myself, *This is interesting!* I knew that because of the Cold War,[2] thousands of soldiers were spread out in US Army bases across West Germany. Our teams had been ministering at several of their locations. We knew there were problems with discipline, morale, and drug addiction. They really did need prayer.

"God Wants Us to Do It!"

We started praying first for many soldiers to receive the gospel. Then we prayed someone would provide Bibles for all the military. Another person spoke up. "I believe God wants someone to give one hundred thousand Bibles to the US military."

Now we had a real, tangible goal.

Our excitement increased as we continued to pray. We became convinced God wanted *us* to get involved.

The name of Dr. Kenneth Taylor, editor of *The Living Bible*, popped into my mind. I thought my friend Brother Andrew might know him. Known as "God's Smuggler," Andrew had taken more than one million Bibles into communist nations and other restricted countries.

After our prayer time ended, I phoned Andrew in the Netherlands and asked how to contact Dr. Taylor. He said, "Come over to my house! Dr. Taylor will be with us this Saturday."

However, Andrew called me back that afternoon. "Sorry, Loren, Dr. Taylor has to return to Chicago on urgent business tomorrow."

He gave me Dr. Taylor's phone number in Athens, Greece. I called and we agreed to meet the next day in the Frankfurt Airport, where he had a two-hour layover.

"How Did You Come Up with That Number?"

Remember, our prayer meeting in Switzerland happened on Monday. The next day I was meeting with Dr. Taylor. I told him how God had led us to pray for the troops in Germany and the idea to give one hundred thousand Bibles to the GIs.

"How did you come up with that number?" he asked.

I told him God put it in our minds.

After a few more questions Dr. Taylor said, "I just happen to have one hundred thousand copies of *The Living Bible* left over from a Billy Graham crusade." He said he would give them to us. But he added that it cost him six dollars to print each Bible.

We in YWAM received a $600,000 gift after ninety minutes of prayer, a couple of phone calls, and a hurried trip from Lausanne to Frankfurt.

Dr. Taylor said we would have to pay to ship the Bibles from Chicago to Germany. I knew they were big, heavy ones. It would cost us a fortune. But I said, "Yes, of course." God had been with us so far, and we would continue to trust him.

On the same day I phoned Colonel Jim Ammerman, who lived in Frankfurt. I shared my vision with him and told him about our prayer time in Lausanne and God's dramatic provision.

"We'll Put Our Green Trucks to Use"

"Your timing is amazing, Loren," Colonel Ammerman said. "Tomorrow all the generals are meeting here in Frankfurt. They've asked me to give a devotional."

He said none of the generals knew the Lord. Then he asked me to take his place speaking to them. "First, you tell them the gospel, Loren. Then tell them your vision of giving Bibles to all the troops."

On Wednesday, two days after our prayer meeting, I preached to the generals. I ended with the plan to offer *The Living Bible* to the soldiers.

The top general agreed to help. "We'll put our green trucks to use!"

Soon soldiers were picking up the hefty packages in Illinois and transporting them to ships and planes. The air force, navy, and army delivered the Bibles to all the US military bases in Germany.

YWAM volunteers, no matter what their nationality, were able to go onto the bases and give away one hundred thousand Bibles.

It didn't stop there. A Christian who coordinated public communication at the Pentagon ordered Scripture readings over the intercom of every base's mess hall at breakfast, lunch, and dinner. They did this for the entire time of the Bible distribution.

From Zero Believers to Many

Now, thirty-one years later at my dad's funeral, Colonel Ammerman told how the Bible distribution led to changes in the military leadership. "When I first became head chaplain, we sent out questionnaires across the world to all American officers, from majors to generals. We asked them, 'Do you know Jesus Christ personally?' Almost no officers professed a saving faith in Jesus. That was before 1972. We just sent out another questionnaire in 2002 to all majors, colonels, and generals. There was an amazing percentage of officers who said they had a personal saving knowledge of Jesus." Colonel Ammerman looked me in the eye. "Loren, when we followed up with those, the vast majority said they came to know Jesus in Germany in the 1970s, when the Bibles were given out."

This can happen again, but in every sphere of society. We must pray, wait on God for his ideas, then take steps of faith.

4

The Bible and Seismic Changes

In the summer of 2014 I stood outside a darkened Wartburg Castle in Germany. I was with a small group of YWAM missionaries, including Suse Schmell, our leader in Bad Blankenburg. She pointed to a rampart with a single lighted window. Suse said that was the cramped room where Martin Luther had translated the Bible into German.

He had escaped to this castle because the authorities were trying to kill him. During his confinement he suffered many dark days of depression. However, Luther said he "fought the devil with ink." He completed his translation of the New Testament in eleven weeks—record time!

His Bible in the language of the people changed Western Europe dramatically. Soon translators completed God's Word in another nineteen European languages. According to Indian philosopher Vishal Mangalwadi, those Bibles shaped our world and created the soul of Western civilization.[1]

I agree with my friend Vishal.

Because Gutenberg had already invented the printing press in Europe, the price of Bibles fell.

Because this new, cheaper version was available in the common languages, people wanted to learn to read.

Because of this demand, communities started schools.

Because of the increase of knowledge, individuals invented technologies that created a stronger base for commerce. New ideas and information spread to the masses, strengthening the middle class and opening further opportunities.

Nature and the Word of God

Many think science and faith in God cannot coexist. According to Vishal Mangalwadi, however, pioneers of modern science depended on the two pillars of truth: nature and the Word of God.[2] Most pioneers of science founded their lives on the Word of God.

Sir Francis Bacon and Galileo Galilei, known as the fathers of modern science, were earnest believers. So were Nicolaus Copernicus, Johannes Kepler, and Isaac Newton.[3]

Scientist René Descartes, a French mathematician, scientist, and philosopher, sought to prove "the near certainty of the existence of God—for only if God both exists and would not want us to be deceived by our experiences, can we trust our senses and logical thought processes."[4]

Even today a significant number of modern scientists believe the Bible. A recent survey showed two million out of twelve million American scientists call themselves "evangelical."[5]

Biblical Faith Led to Great Art

The arts also flourished as more people read the Bible. Stories in God's Word have inspired some of the most talented people the world has ever known. Whether you're gazing up at Michelangelo's ceiling in the Sistine Chapel or at Rembrandt's portrait of himself helping to crucify Jesus, or studying the faces and postures of the disciples in Leonardo da Vinci's *The Last Supper*, you are seeing the result of faith and devotion.

Scripture also led to great music. A devout composer, George Frideric Handel wrote the *Messiah* based entirely on Bible portions about Jesus. When Handel finished the "Hallelujah Chorus," he said, "I did think I did see all Heaven before me, and the great God Himself."[6]

Handel faced fierce opposition. Organized religion was outraged that the words of God were being spoken in a theater. He performed his sacred oratorio only once in a church—Bristol Cathedral. John Wesley attended that night and said afterward, "I doubt if that congregation was ever so serious at a sermon as they were during this performance."[7]

Johann Sebastian Bach was also a deeply committed Christian. He signed each piece of music with "S.D.G.," meaning *Soli Deo gloria*—"For the glory of God alone."

Seismic Changes from the "Priesthood of Believers"

Sweeping changes came because people read the Bible. The Reformers, starting with Luther, emphasized the "priesthood of all believers."[8] Of course, he found this teaching in several places in Scripture. God wanted his people to be a nation of priests.[9] According to Martin Luther, this meant everyone had a calling. There was no division between the sacred and the secular. Whether serving as full-time clergy or plowboys, everyone should consider their job sacred.

It followed that if God declared all Christians priests, they should be able to read. Literacy and education grew in Western Europe, not just for the elite or special classes, but for everyone. That is the principal reason the West continues to lead the world in education today, five hundred years later.

New creativity, excellence, and integrity in commerce grew out of this idea of doing work as unto the Lord. It birthed our modern economy, along with democratic governments. If we are equal before God and responsible to him, we must hold our rulers accountable. No one is above the law. Everyone is valuable because we are all made in the image of God.

Some may point out that democracy began earlier. Yes, in ancient Greece some elite men of society were able to vote. This was true also when King John of England was forced to sign the Magna Carta. It only allowed the elite to vote. That event in 1215 was the first opening bud on the tree of liberty. After the Reformation it bloomed into full flower.

All from a Cramped Room in Wartburg Castle

I don't often feel like an American. YWAM's international ministry has staff living in 191 nations. My full-time coworkers come from more than two hundred sovereign nations and countries. Working with this incredible team makes me feel more like a citizen of the world than an American.

Yet the United States was the nation of my birth. America stands out because of its beginnings. Its founding fathers deliberately grounded their new nation in Scripture.

Modern secularists and atheists have tried to erase America's Christian foundations.[10] At the end of the nineteenth century, however, the US Supreme Court commissioned a ten-year study of five hundred documents of the nation's founders. They looked for the predominant philosophy behind the American Revolution. The court declared, "[America is] a Christian people, and the morality of the country is deeply engrafted upon Christianity."[11]

A recent study of fifteen thousand documents of the fifty-five authors of the US Constitution discovered that 34 percent of their quotations came straight from the Bible. Another 60 percent of their quotations came from writers who used the Bible to form their conclusions. Thus, 94 percent of the founding fathers' quotes were based directly or indirectly on Scripture.[12]

The framers of the US Constitution absorbed the Word of God. Their ideas for democracy were based partly on Martin Luther's emphasis on the priesthood of all believers.

Were there flaws among the founding fathers? Yes. For instance, some of them were abolitionists actively opposed to slavery. Yet they compromised their convictions in order to bring Southern colonies into the new country, colonies whose economies were based on slavery.

A few decades later, however, Americans went to war over this omission. Roughly 2 percent of America—620,000 men—died in the conflict that gave slaves their freedom.[13]

It was the only time in history that a country went to war to end slavery. America isn't the only example of a country that has Christian foundations. Examples abound of countries in which a godly minority studied and obeyed the Word of God. These minorities brought social, political, and economic improvements to their nations.[14]

You could say all this transformation—science, economic development, education, art, music, and democracy—flowed from that cramped little room in Wartburg Castle. That's where a priest in hiding translated the Bible into the language of the common people.

5

We Can Do It

Taking the Good Book to every home on the planet presents a huge challenge. But we, the body of Christ, can do it with the help of God. With God all things are possible. He has shown us in three ways that he is behind this effort, speeding us toward the goal. The first sign is unprecedented unity in the body of Christ.

Two Popes and an Archbishop

The body of Christ has been severely divided for nearly one thousand years, following the schism between Orthodox and Catholic Christians.[1] It split again during the Reformation five hundred years ago. I know some may find this hard to believe because of the deep wounds, but today the Lord is mending centuries of division among his followers.

Recently, David Hamilton, my wife Darlene, and I met with

ten significant leaders in ten days. We saw some of the ways God is working to bring Christians together.

It began when I was praying about ending Bible poverty. John 10:1 came to mind: "Anyone who does not enter the sheep pen by the gate, but climbs in by some other way, is a thief and a robber." I took this as God's instruction for our first steps to end Bible poverty. We should seek the blessing of Christian leaders on this effort, thus "going in by the sheep gate" and not climbing over a wall.

We decided to seek appointments with leaders from all segments of Christianity—Orthodox, Anglican, Catholic, and many Protestant leaders. We knew we had significant links to each of these leaders through YWAM staff. We contacted our coworkers, and within a day or two we had appointments with Pope Tawadros II of the Coptic Orthodox Church, which is the oldest Christian tradition; Justin Welby, archbishop of Canterbury and symbolic head of Anglicans and Episcopalians worldwide; and Pope Francis, leader of 1.2 billion Roman Catholics.

We also met with major evangelical leaders, such as the founders of the Alpha Course, Nicky and Pippa Gumbel. We shared with the heads of various Bible societies and pastors of megachurches, such as Rick Warren. In just ten days' time we got appointments with ten significant leaders on three continents, seeking their blessings on the effort to end Bible poverty now.

I have continued ever since, seeking out heads of ministries to get their blessings on the efforts to end Bible poverty.

Table 71

Decades ago God began stirring missionary groups to work together to complete the Great Commission.[2] In 1974 Dr. Billy

Graham gathered Christians for that purpose. The first World Congress on Evangelization took place in Lausanne that year. I was privileged to speak at one of the breakout sessions.

Throughout the following years, the Billy Graham Association convened other gatherings, pulling together heads of large and small missions. Amsterdam 2000 was one of those times. It drew thousands of leaders from all over the world. Organizers of the conference invited several hundred people to meet separately in a working group. They were to determine what it will take to finish the Great Commission. Some from YWAM were in this working group.

For several days, representatives of missionary movements sat at seventy-five small tables discussing how to complete the job Jesus gave us. Members of some of the largest missions were sitting at table 71.

At the front, Paul Eshleman, founder of the Jesus Film Project, challenged everyone to take on the untargeted, unreached people groups. Bruce Wilkinson, author of *The Prayer of Jabez*, stood up and said, "The fact that there are *untargeted* people groups means we're not doing our job!" He went on to say that the leaders of the vast majority of Christian missionaries were in that room. "We can decide today if we want to do it."

They Came Weeping

Mark Anderson was one of the YWAMers there. He says emotions were building around the tables, particularly as they realized the Lord had already given them all they needed to finish evangelizing the world.

On the third day of the working group, Eshleman stood and urged the attendees to find others from their contingent in the room. "Get together now and decide what the Lord wants you to do. Then come over here and shake my hand, telling me what groups you will adopt." There were several hundred groups of untargeted, unreached *ethnē* with populations of at least one hundred thousand.

People began coming up to Eshleman, choosing one, two, or three groups. The Holy Spirit was quietly stirring them. Some came weeping and embracing others. Something was breaking through in the heavenlies.

The total adopted people groups came to approximately 140—*ethnē* who were about to hear the name of Jesus for the first time!

Then people stopped coming forward.

The room grew quiet. Disappointment hung heavy in the air. Who would reach the remaining groups?

We Can Go In, but We Might Not Come Out

Mark Anderson was sitting at table 71 along with Steve Douglass of Cru.[3] Steve leaned over. "Why don't our two organizations—YWAM and Cru—finish it?" It was a startling commitment. The remaining groups lived in the world's most dangerous places. We could go in, but we might not come out. Still, the two groups agreed to adopt them.

All those at table 71 began to strategize, deciding on the basic elements of evangelism—church planting, discipleship, and Bible translation and distribution. As they came to each component, they thought of who should be at the table. They would need Bibles, so they called Roy Peterson over. He was head of Wycliffe at that time. They needed church planters. That's why they asked Avery Willis from the Southern Baptists to join in.

Target: Zero

Finally, they wrote up a covenant to reach the number zero, meaning that someday soon there would be zero unreached people groups. If they searched all over the world, no one would be able to find a group that hadn't heard the gospel.

Each leader signed the covenant.

Those clustered there decided to call themselves "Table 71." As the meetings continued in Amsterdam, these veteran missionaries went into overtime. They met during breaks. They worked early and late. And they kept meeting after the conference finished.

Now Table 71 gets together several times a year to pray and plan. They've invited others to join them, those who are known for various components of the task. Table 71 is made up of seventeen missions, some from the largest missionary organizations, including YWAM. Our contribution is thousands of young recruits eager to be out on the front lines.

I've been privileged to sit in with Table 71 on a number of occasions, especially when they meet at our University of the Nations campus in Kona. They encourage each other, share data, give financially from one mission to another, and commit to various aspects of finishing the Great Commission.

They have worked steadily. During the first ten years, Table 71 spurred missions movements to plant churches. As of the writing of this book, YWAM and our sister movements have planted fourteen thousand new churches. Pastors have baptized more than one hundred thousand people. These congregations are now sending out their own missionaries to other untargeted groups.

Table 71's team members have become dear friends, evidence of unity the Lord has brought about. The Holy Spirit is free to empower us when we are united (Ps. 133:1–2). He's giving us strength to accomplish the greatest job ever given.

Strategic ministries have joined the ranks of those committed to obeying Christ's last command. For example, more than twelve hundred leaders of missionary organizations and denominations are meeting at call2all conferences all over the world. Their purpose is to collaborate and focus on finishing the Great Commission.

6

Technologies to Speed the Word

We've seen that the first way God is helping us spread his Word is through unprecedented unity in the body of Christ. The second way is through new technology. You might not be interested in technology, or it may intimidate you a bit. But we must all thank the Lord for these amazing developments and take part in using these tools. The internet has been used for horrific things like pornography, sex trafficking, and terrorism. But I am convinced that the Lord allowed innovations to be developed because of their potential to spread the gospel worldwide.

Let me tell you a story from Nepal. One of our gifted leaders in that country is named Dilli. He was a Brahmin training to become a Hindu priest. But then he met Jesus and joined YWAM. A few years later when Dilli heard my message on ending Bible poverty, he went right to work. He made a plan to get God's Word to every home in his nation.

Dax Fears, along with several other young people from our Kona campus, got wind of Dilli's plan. They started strategizing how they could end Bible poverty in Nepal, gathering there in September 2015. By then Dilli was leading Nepal's interdenominational ministers' alliance. These pastors heard about ending Bible poverty and also wanted to be a part of it.

Dilli and Jeremy,[1] a team leader, assigned those from YWAM Kona a certain area of Nepal (unnamed for security reasons). Dax and nine other young men flew to this distant region high in the Himalayas, landing on a bumpy airfield. From there they trekked for days into the mountains.

They were headed into an impoverished region even the hardy Nepalis consider remote. The first village sat at an altitude of twelve thousand feet (3,657 meters). Yet the team of ten missionaries carried more than one hundred Bibles in each of their backpacks, in addition to their gear and supplies. How could they do this while climbing in high altitudes? Because of technology.

The team carried microSD cards the size of the nail on your little finger. The cards fit inside smartphones and each one held the *Jesus* film as well as an audio Bible in the Nepali language. The team also carried about forty printed Bibles for those who could read. Because of government surveys, plus the work of Dilli and the Nepali pastors, they knew the number of homes in their three target villages, as well as how many people were literate.

Smartphones at Twelve Thousand Feet

In the first village, just over the summit of a mountain, a woman greeted them. Her face was leathery from a lifetime of harsh wind and cold, but her voice was warm and friendly. *"Jaimasi!"*

she exclaimed. The team instantly recognized her as a Christian since she didn't say *"namaste,"* the usual Hindu greeting.

When Jeremy, who spoke fluent Nepali, explained why they had come, she grinned broadly and motioned them into her home.

As the team crowded in, Dax looked around. The woman's wood stove stood with its door propped open. That explained the gray and black smoke stains coloring the walls and ceiling. She stuffed more wood into the fire, then placed pots atop the stove to make dinner.

Later as they ate rice and beans, Jeremy asked if she had a Bible. She brought out an ancient copy and proudly handed it to one of the team. Jeremy learned she was unable to read.

She said, "I only get to hear the Bible when my daughter visits. She can't come that often because of her work in the city."

The team gave the woman a device containing an audio Bible. As she listened to God's Word in her language, her eyes grew wide and filled with tears. It was the most precious gift they could give her.

On this test run the team covered three villages in four days. A small fraction of people turned them down. The majority eagerly received Bibles.

Thirty-One Bibles Every Three Minutes

Now many YWAM teams go to Nepal each year, including twenty or more teams from Kona. One of our teams trekked more than one hundred miles round-trip to reach a remote village.

These volunteers are working closely with Dilli and local pastors. They use recent government surveys to determine the literacy rate and the number of households in each area. Then they carefully track their progress.

To ensure a supply of audio Bibles, YWAM Kona bought a machine that copies data onto microSD cards. Each card contains an audio Bible and the *Jesus* film. The machine produces these "tiny Bibles" at a rate of thirty-one every three minutes.

Innovations to Help End Bible Poverty

MicroSD cards are just one example of technology the Lord is using to speed up the task. There are many others.

- Millions can download Bibles in closed nations via the internet.[2]
- Norwegian YWAMers are working with an app designer on a device to track households and their response to the Bibles.[3]
- Elon Musk, a founder of Tesla, is exploring the possibility of using seven hundred cheaper satellites to deliver wireless internet to the entire world.[4] Mission groups are ready to use these or other satellites to offer verbal Bibles worldwide.

Solar-Powered Projector + Bedsheet = Theater for 1,000

Believers such as David Palusky are also inventing new technologies. David is an electrical engineer. He and his wife, Stephanie, began Renew World Outreach to help missionaries use technology to get God's Word to remote people groups. Their IT (information technology) tools also help disciple these tribes.

The Paluskys made several mission trips to an unengaged people group on the banks of the Amazon River in Peru. The tribal chief pleaded with them. "Can you help us? We have the Bible in our mother tongue, but no one knows how to read."

So David invented his first device, called the Vista. It's a sturdy, solar-powered projector system. It plays the *Jesus* film, which is 80 percent of the Gospel of Luke, as well as other gospel films. It runs on a solar-charged battery, or by plugging into an outlet. It projects the film on a wall, portable screen, or even a bedsheet. The sound can carry to one thousand people. Yet a single person can easily transport it and set it up.[5]

Renew World Outreach continues to create innovations to help end Bible poverty. Another of their technological tools is called the LightStream. It's a portable media distribution system that allows access to free verbal and print Bibles on mobile devices. Think of it as a portable Wi-Fi hotspot. It transmits to fifteen people nearby, offering them verbal and text Bibles, movies such as the *Jesus* film, and other audio gospel training materials. It's all in their language and done without internet or electricity.[6]

What's more, those who receive this transmission can then share the Bibles and movies with their friends via email, Bluetooth, or social media. Their friends can then share it with their friends, and their friends' friends.

What an amazing way to distribute Bibles!

Imagine yourself in a restricted-access country, sitting in a mall or park, inviting people to stream free Bibles in their language—without connecting to the internet! In such countries, distribution of printed Bibles or contact via the internet could mean imprisonment or death for the recipient. The distributor could go to prison as well. But someone quietly downloading a Bible has less chance of being discovered.

Another mission focusing on high tech is Faith Comes By Hearing. They have been putting verbal Bibles into the hands of people around the globe for decades. They started with cassette players. Now they have an outstanding team of IT experts creating cutting-edge digital tools. They also have verbal recordings of the Bible in more than one thousand languages. As of right now, forty-two national teams are working in twenty-seven locations around the world, completing a new language recording every three days.

Ululations in Denny's

Faith Comes By Hearing developed a smartphone app called "Bible.is." It contains verbal Bibles in 916 languages. The app also contains 1,029 translations of Bibles in text form and the *Jesus* film dubbed into more than one thousand languages. Users can search by version, language, or country to access the Scriptures.

Morgan Jackson is a leader in Faith Comes By Hearing. One of his many remarkable stories involves this app. It shows how Bible distribution is not just about illiterate, unreached people groups high in the Himalayas or deep in the Amazon jungle. The unreached can be right in your hometown.

Morgan went to lunch at a Denny's restaurant in Pasadena, California. He noticed his waitress spoke English with a foreign accent. It was lunch hour and the place was packed. When he finished his meal, the waitress dashed over and dropped off the check with a "Bless you," then bolted to another table.

"Wait! Wait!" Morgan called after her.

"Anything wrong, sir?"

"I noticed your accent. Where are you from?"

"Ethiopia."

Morgan opened his smartphone and selected the Bible.is app. He touched a button and the app revealed a choice of twenty-four Ethiopian languages. "What is your mother tongue?"

"Tigrinya."

Not only did the app have a verbal Bible in Tigrinya, but a small icon showed the device also contained the *Jesus* film in her language. Morgan chose the verbal Bible, then pressed "play" and handed the phone to his waitress.

She listened, then began ululating—a piercing wail of strong emotion. Startled customers looked their way. She looked at the screen and cried out again. And again.

Morgan asked what she was doing. She told him she was blessing him according to tribal tradition. "This is the happiest day of my life! If they fire me for doing this, it's okay. My religion is more important."

Morgan quickly explained that she didn't have to lose her job. He asked for her mobile phone number, then hit "share" on Bible.is.

She was so excited that she pulled another waitress over. She was from Indonesia. Morgan shared the app, giving the second waitress the Javanese verbal and text Bibles plus the *Jesus* film.

Morgan did all this—leaving both waitresses with the Bible app in their mother tongue—all before he paid for his meal.

7

The Greatest Spread
of the Bible in History

Twenty-one percent of Americans speak a language other than English in their home. If you get Bible.is on your smartphone, you can offer God's Word to anyone. In almost every instance, you will find people open and excited to have Scripture in the language of their heart. That's why Faith Comes By Hearing has hundreds of millions of users over their digital devices. These users are accessing digital, verbal, and braille Bibles, in addition to video signage for the deaf in twenty sign languages.

These stories come from only two of the missions using technology to spread God's Word. More than 140 Bible societies, the Jesus Film Project, Wycliffe, the Seed Company, SIL, YWAM, and many more are working to end Bible poverty. More become involved with technology every day.

There isn't time or space to tell all that is happening.

Time of Ignorance, Time of Hope

Despite the remarkable spread of the Bible into new languages, ignorance of what the Bible says is growing among the general public. Countries that have had the Bible for centuries now show a lack of biblical knowledge.

In Norway, YWAMers engaged in ending Bible poverty asked a polling service to do a survey. To our workers' surprise, the pollsters found that 30 percent of Norwegians had no Bible in their homes.

Every school in America used to have daily prayer and Bible reading. The US Supreme Court ended that practice by a ruling in 1962. Since then, drugs, alcohol, gang violence, and shootings have replaced God's Word and prayer in schools. Now the education level of America among the nations has plummeted from the top ranking down to number twenty-eight worldwide. Twenty-seven countries do better at educating their children than the United States does.[1]

Lack of Bible training in the general public has produced astounding results. Bible ignorance continues to worsen. The Supreme Court's ruling in 1962 has been stretched to ridiculous measures. Educators and city officials now ban anything religious in public spaces. They are frightened by militant atheists who seem to have unlimited money for lawsuits. The following story shows how extreme some atheists have become.

"Someone Might Be Offended"

Christina Zavala, a mother in Palmdale, California, began enclosing an inspirational note along with a Bible verse each day in her seven-year-old son's lunchbox. His friends read the notes and were soon clamoring for more. His teacher learned about the popularity of these notes and reprimanded the boy in front of his class. He came home in tears.

The situation escalated from there. The principal told Zavala that her son could only give out his Bible verses after school, off school property. Zavala complied, and still the boy's gospel notes grew in popularity. Students went out of their way to find him.

Then one day a Los Angeles deputy sheriff knocked on Zavala's door. He demanded the little boy stop sharing his notes altogether. He said, "Someone might be offended."[2]

No wonder ignorance of God's Word has grown. According to a Pew survey, more than half of Americans cannot name the four Gospels in order. A troubling number of Christians doubt the book of Genesis is true. The average churchgoer may not even know who Abraham or Moses were.[3]

Many churches provide scant Bible training for their members. I preach in numerous services each year in twenty to forty countries. I have noticed that congregations spend as much as an hour in worship through singing but only have a twenty-minute sermon.

For the majority, that's the only Bible training they get all week. How many churches in your city or suburb still have Sunday school classes? Small home groups have largely replaced adult Sunday school classes. But these groups can be limited, often centered on fellowship, encouragement, and a discussion about a certain topic rather than the comprehensive Bible studies typical of traditional Sunday school classes.

The Great Contradiction

Meanwhile there is a growing hunger for the Word of God.

Jesus predicted this polarization. He said many will turn from the truth (Matt. 24:10). But the Word of God also says the knowledge of the glory of God will fill the earth like the oceans (Hab. 2:14). If we focus only on one side of this great contradiction, the one that fills us with dread, we will lose hope and our faith will suffer. But if we look at how God is preparing people to receive his Word, our faith will mount up.

Two examples from the entertainment industry show that the American public is open to the Bible. Scripture-based movies and television series were such a success in 2014 that Hollywood called it "The Year of the Bible." Roma Downey and her husband, Mark Burnett, did a series for the History Channel called *The Bible*. It drew the largest viewing audience on basic cable that year. In the next two years, Downey and Burnett followed with two other blockbusters: *Son of God* and *A.D., The Bible Continues*.

In 1995–96 Svein Tindberg, a well-known actor in Norway, memorized the Gospel of Mark. He did a three-hour, one-man stage performance with a chair and a desk as his only props. The response was huge. Seventy-five thousand people attended the performances. That box office is even more significant when you consider the population of Norway is about the same as Singapore, a little over five million. Tindberg followed up his success in 2000 with a new show, reciting the book of Acts. He packed out theaters wherever he performed.[4]

First the Bible, Then Revival

Our YWAM teams have encountered unprecedented openness in countless places, including America and other Western countries. But they've also encountered outright hostility. This is to be expected. Several men and women of God have prophesied that persecution is coming, but also that the greatest spiritual awakening the world has ever seen is on its way.

As I have studied historical moves of God I've found they are always preceded by immersion in the Bible. Someone sows the seed of God's Word beforehand.

However, one great exception puzzled me: the 1960s awakenings in West Timor, Indonesia. Thousands converted to Christianity in a Muslim country.[5] Yet a leading preacher in that move of God said there was no emphasis on Scripture.

Then I met a veteran Swiss-German missionary couple, the Germanides. They left West Timor two years before the awakening began. I asked them about what the preacher said, that there was no spreading of the Bible ahead of time.

Mr. Germanide replied, "No. That's not true. My wife and I spent twelve years going to every home in West Timor, giving out Bibles."

Throughout history, spiritual awakenings have needed three things: exposure to Scripture, active witnesses, and encounters with a living God.

English evangelist Smith Wigglesworth gave a dramatic prophecy in 1947: "When the Word and the Spirit come together, there will be the biggest movement of the Holy Spirit that [the UK], and indeed the world, has ever seen."[6]

We live in a time of unprecedented acceleration of Bible distribution to every country and every people group. Is it possible to reach every household in this generation? Yes! I believe it is. And it will prepare the way for the greatest spiritual awakening in history. We are going to see Habakkuk's vision become reality (Hab. 2:14).

8

How to End Bible Poverty

We've talked about electronic breakthroughs making it easier and faster to take God's Word to everyone. But the biggest means to end Bible poverty isn't new. It's thousands of years old. It's prayer, particularly the kind that listens for guidance from the Lord and obeys him.

Jesus said he only did what he saw the Father doing (John 5:19). He lived this out from the beginning, praying and seeking the Father's guidance. Before he chose the twelve disciples, he prayed all night. If Jesus needed to be in constant communication with God the Father, how much more do we need it?

He also told his disciples their prayers would change the world. He told them how to pray. "May your Kingdom come soon. May your will be done on earth, as it is in heaven" (Matt. 6:10 NLT). He asks us to pray that same prayer today—not as a ritual but as an urgent plea. He wants his will to be done on earth, and he asks us to intercede for that.

We must be vigilant. The god of this world hates God's Word. He fears it and the power of our prayers. He's determined to oppose us at every turn. He will use criticism, misunderstanding, division, ridicule, slander, lawsuits, financial repercussions, government opposition, and physical attacks. We must not be ignorant of his devices but battle spiritual forces in Jesus' name until we defeat them.

This is why the first step in ending Bible poverty is continuous, Holy Spirit-led prayer. Our goal in YWAM is to rally at least one million people to sign the pledge to pray every day for the End Bible Poverty Now vision. We need people who will intercede, then obey whatever the Lord tells them to do.[1]

Knocking on the Sheep Gate

Next, we must get the blessing of Christian leaders. As I said earlier, when we were asking the Lord where to begin, he said to me, "John 10." Remember, the first verse of that chapter says the true shepherd enters by the door. Anyone who climbs in some other way is a thief and a robber.

Jesus was talking about himself as the Shepherd in this passage. But since the Lord gave me that reference, I knew he was using it to remind me of the "Sheep Gate Principle." That means we should start by contacting Christian leaders.

I am continuing to "knock on the sheep gate" by introducing other leaders to this project. You can do this too, whether you give out Bibles in your town, your nation, or halfway around the world. Wherever possible, seek the blessing of church leaders.

We also need endorsements from other authorities. We must call on believers in every sphere of society to help end Bible poverty.

The Man or Woman of Peace

It's important to keep our goals simple. If our focus is on Jesus and the Bible, we'll find it easy to get the blessing of the shepherds. We don't have the luxury of side issues or differences of opinion. If we get sidetracked we won't finish the task. It's only about Jesus. It's only about God's Word.

We accomplished this in Hawai'i in 1983. We took out ads, appeared on statewide television, sought interviews with local newspapers, and spoke in churches. We received endorsements from Catholic, Protestant, and Jewish leaders.

The more we enter through the sheep gate by seeking the blessing of leaders, the greater the public response will be as we distribute Bibles.

Besides the Sheep Gate Principle, Jesus gave another guideline for ministries, especially mobile ones. We are to seek out the man or woman of peace for a specific geographical area. This idea is based on a phrase from Luke 10:6, when Jesus sent seventy disciples on a short-term mission. We've observed this principle since the earliest days of YWAM, relying on the Lord to lead us to such a person when going into an unfamiliar place.

As you'll recall, the woman of peace in St. Thomas was Miss Armstrong. She opened many doors for us in her community, including housing, ministry opportunities, and promotion through local media.

If you feel the Spirit calling you to end Bible poverty in your community, whether it's a city high-rise or a rural village, ask the Lord to lead you to the right people. Seek God for the most effective approach.

Don't forget to communicate with us, so we can know of progress toward ending Bible poverty. Write to Dax Fears at the YWAM Kona Bible Office (KonaBibleTeam@gmail.com and the website Bibles.global). Let us know when you are starting, and what you are aiming to do. Give praise reports along the way, any stories you want to share, or prayer requests to pass along. And be sure to tell us when you finish your goal.

Make It a Christmas Gift, Have a Party

Ending Bible poverty isn't a one-size-fits-all project. There's room for Spirit-led creativity and initiative. Ask the Lord's guidance for each step. He has the most creativity of all, and he knows your community better than you do. He will give you just the right slant for them.

You might hand out gift-wrapped Bibles in your neighborhood at Christmas. Or you could give Bibles during the week before Easter.

Follow up your distribution with an open block party, perhaps on a Friday evening. Serve dessert and coffee and have more Bibles available for people to give to others. A short reading of a Bible passage can open things up for discussion. Then announce the opportunity for a regular group meeting, going through God's Word at your house, or during lunchtime at your workplace or school. Make it about personal relations, not about an institution.

We must be methodical, using government statistics and data to locate homes in specific target areas and, where needed, to determine the mother tongue of each household. We did that in Hawai'i in 1983 and gave Bibles in the fifteen languages spoken in the islands to every home.

Not long before the writing of this book, several mission groups began to research, map, and plan together for distribution in various countries, working in cities, on far-flung islands of the Pacific, and in high mountain villages of Asia.

Another way we're tracking language needs is through the

Bible Poverty Index, created by 4K Mapping team headed by Jill Thornton in August 2016.[2]

The Omega Zones

One of the great implements for the mapping of missionary efforts is the concept of "Omega Zones." This is a framework of data arranged to break gigantic nations into smaller units, while also targeting tiny countries on the map. This collection of data and maps is called "4K" because the entire world is divided into approximately four thousand zones. Even something as huge as the task of world evangelization can be made more manageable by breaking it into small sections. Missionary movements, churches, and volunteer groups are using this strategic map to help fulfill the Great Commission.

This strategy was developed at the beginning of the twenty-first century, when David Hamilton set out to create a new world map for missionary outreach—one that would help believers zero in on areas of great need.

Many joined him in this new challenge. His team included Jill Thornton, who brought her knowledge of research and cartography, as well as others with specialized skills in research, cartography, design, and web development. Together they put thousands of hours into this effort. I was honored to name these zones. I chose "Omega" because it is one of the names of Jesus. As the final letter of the Greek alphabet, it also symbolizes the completion or finishing of the task of evangelization.

The zones are based on population and political boundaries. For instance, a country like China is broken into 857 Omega Zones, while Samoa and its two hundred thousand people are one Omega Zone. The zones are also based on the availability of the gospel in a nation or province. Still another criteria of

Omega Zones is hard to define. I call it the element of personal identity.

For example, if someone asks me where I'm from, I say, "California." If they press me further I say, "Los Angeles." But where in Los Angeles? I'll answer, "West LA." Because those are my roots. It's my early sense of belonging, an emotional thing. This element is also considered in the division of Omega Zones.

The 4K team is constantly researching and updating the Omega Zones to reflect the needs of people across the globe. Hundreds of other missions are now working with the 4K Omega Zones and sharing their map data so that all missionaries can have a clearer view of needs around the world. Those collaborating in this research include the Jesus Film Project, Finishing the Task, SIL International, Wycliffe's Global Alliance, Cru, YWAM, and various others.

Above the Arctic Circle

YWAM workers in Norway took up the task of ending Bible poverty and ran with it. Joakim Magnus said, "We heard Loren's vision about the Bibles. That decided it for us. It was a vision from God. We needed to do this."

Their distribution started in Finnmark, an area of Norway above the Arctic Circle. I joined the teams for a couple of days as they walked from home to home. We visited houses scattered across the tundra in the sparsely populated zone. We offered Bibles in Norwegian or Scripture portions in Sami, the language of Laplanders. The latter expressed indifference to Norwegian Bibles but grabbed the Sami ones.

YWAM leader Hans Sandtorp is working on an app to track Bible distribution. It will pinpoint neighborhoods and homes that are unreached, as well as the primary language of each household. When a group or individual commits to distributing Bibles, the app will show unreached neighborhoods. Finally, it records every home that has been contacted. As of the publication of this book, Hans is still working on this system.

Meanwhile, in Latvia

During the Cold War between Western democracies and Eastern communist nations, YWAM missionaries Al and Carolyn Akimoff ministered behind the Iron Curtain.[3] People who lived under the thumb of Marxism could be imprisoned or worse if they were caught having an unregistered religious meeting. The same could happen to Western visitors trying to help them.

Nevertheless, the Akimoffs regularly went to Iron Curtain countries to hold secret Bible trainings in the forests. They taught crowds of young people about God's nature and character, how to hear the voice of God more clearly, and how to trust him for provision.

One of those whom Al and Carolyn trained was Latvian pastor Petr Samoylich. In the mid-1990s, he began focusing on getting Bibles to schoolchildren and their families by first going to the teachers. Petr has been organizing public school teacher conferences ever since, teaching teachers from all over Latvia.

When I attended his conference recently, two outstanding principals from America came to teach 250 teachers. As I walked into the auditorium the first day, I saw 250 boxes stacked in an odd configuration on the stage. Someone told me there were ten thousand Bibles in the boxes, and they were stacked to outline a map of Latvia.

Petr also invited the Latvian Catholic cardinal, the Lutheran bishop, and the leader of the Latvian Baptist Church to the conference. Together we blessed the Bibles, dedicating them for public schools and Sunday schools.

Afterward, each teacher took a few Bibles for themselves, the families of their students, their friends, and the principals of their schools. Petr took orders for hundreds of Bibles. He tells me teachers are still receiving Bibles for their students. The teachers' dedication is inspiring. They even slept on concrete floors to attend the conference.

Since the teachers had no way to carry boxes of Bibles home, Petr had a reason to go visit them to deliver the Bibles. When he invited me into his office, I saw his map on the wall. It had brightly colored pushpins scattered all over it, indicating where teachers are distributing Bibles. He says by 2020 every student and every home in Latvia will have been offered a Bible.

Six Ways to End Bible Poverty

Missionaries are already working to end Bible poverty in a number of other nations: Germany, the Netherlands, Costa Rica, the Philippines, Brazil, Papua New Guinea, Cameroon, and the United States, to name a few. The key to finishing this challenge is to pray and then listen to the Lord. He has the most creative ways to do this. Then we must obey whatever he tells us to do.

Ending Bible poverty requires:

- *Prayer.* This is critical for every part of ending Bible poverty. God invites us to create with him, to follow his lead, and to lean forward in faith.
- *Translation in written and verbal forms.* Everyone has the right to have God's Word in the language of their heart. It is a great injustice that multitudes have no Scripture

at all. We must begin translation and have at least a portion of Scripture for every tongue by 2033, the date agreed on by many mission groups, if not sooner.

- *Production.* Every person must have the Bible in the most accessible form possible, including print, digital, verbal, animation, braille, video and more.[4]
- *Distribution.* We need to do whatever we can in groups and as individuals. Giving out Bibles or portions of it should be second nature to us. Now, with microSD cards and apps on our smartphones, we can carry verbal and text Bibles in hundreds of languages everywhere we go.
- *Education.* Using appropriate means for both oral and literate students, we must educate people so they can read, hear, understand, and apply the Scriptures. We must also teach how the Bible transforms individuals, societies, and nations.
- *Engagement.* With God's help we are called to motivate everyone everywhere to engage regularly with God's Word, and to apply it in their lives. This will help bring a global spiritual awakening when the Word and the Spirit come together.

Jesus gave his people this mandate just before he ascended into heaven. It has been the responsibility of every generation since then. Now it is our assignment. Thanks to modern travel and a host of IT capabilities, it's easier and can happen quickly. With the help of the Holy Spirit, the worldwide body of Christ can do this. Sign the commitment online, promising to pray and do everything God shows you to do. Recruit others to do the same. Gather people who will pray with you and follow the principles God has given for this project.

Choose something from the above list of six items. Perhaps you can pray and contribute financially to those translating, producing, and distributing God's Word. You might pass out Bibles in your neighborhood or to those who have been forgotten in hospitals and prisons. Don't relegate this task to the most remote places. People in your own country need Bibles too. Offer another chance to those who have ignored God's Word or have never considered it.

The Lord may also lead you to the farthest parts of the earth, to an *ethnos* that has waited thousands of years for God's precious Word. Let the Lord lead you. You can be part of reaching the last, the least, and the lost.

9

God's Word in Their Heart Language

His name was Opukaha'ia. His story shows how one individual's choices can change an entire country. It was one of the most dramatic instances in the history of ending Bible poverty, and it all started with a Hawaiian teenager.

King Kamehameha was building his kingdom, destroying his rivals in a final drive to unite the islands. Opukaha'ia and his family were unfortunate enough to be under the rule of one of his last opponents. The boy was only ten years old when he watched in horror as King Kamehameha's warriors slaughtered his parents. He put his baby brother on his back and tried to run to safety, but a warrior threw his spear.

Opukaha'ia felt his brother's body go limp. The little one was gone, but he had spared the life of his big brother. For some reason, the warrior decided not to murder Opukaha'ia too. Instead he took him captive.

All of this happened on what's now known as the Big Island, the one named Hawai'i. A few years later, after Opukaha'ia was no longer a captive, he swam out to a New Haven sealing ship anchored in Kealakekua Bay. Captain Caleb Brintnall, a devoted Christian, took on the boy as a sailor. The crew named him Henry Obookiah because they couldn't pronounce Opukaha'ia.

During Henry's two years on board the sealing ship, a Christian sailor began to teach him English. Henry ended up in New Haven, Connecticut. After some weeks of living and working there, he was sitting in dejection on the steps of Yale College. A theology student came along and asked why he was sad. The young immigrant said, "No one give me learning!"

Emerging Heroes

The student, named Edwin Dwight, promised to find Henry a tutor. He asked a distant cousin if he could take in the Hawaiian as a servant. That's how Henry found himself working in the household of Timothy Dwight IV, president of Yale. Dwight was also one of the founders of the American Board of Commissioners for Foreign Missions. As you can see, Yale was quite different than it is today.

Dwight was an influence on the young man in his move toward Jesus and the gospel. Others tutored Henry over five or six years. They discovered him to be a gifted student. The young Hawaiian became proficient in several languages and devised an alphabet for his people. He also began a Hawaiian grammar book and translated the book of Genesis. His goal was to return as a missionary with the Bible in the language of his people.[1]

At the time a missions movement was growing out of the Second Great Awakening in the United States. Groups of young people met to pray fervently. They eagerly followed emerging heroes like Henry Opukaha'ia. He spoke in colleges and churches, urging young people to help him take the gospel to his homeland. The future looked bright for Henry.

Then Henry contracted typhus and died quickly. He was about thirty years old.

Before he died, Henry wrote a brief story of his life. After his death Edwin Dwight, the theology student who had found him on the steps of Yale years before, compiled *The Memoirs of Henry Obookiah* using Henry's own story, a collection of his letters, and Dwight's observations. That book and the news of his death spread all over New England, touching the hearts of young people. Seven missionary couples and three Hawaiian young men decided to take Henry's place and sail to Hawai'i.

The Small, Black Box

They brought with them a printing press and Henry's Hawaiian alphabet, grammar book, and translation of the book of Genesis.

They sailed south from New England, all the way down the length of North and South America, around Cape Horn, up the length of South America again, and finally across the Pacific for about 6,800 miles to Hawai'i. It took them 164 days. On the high seas they had no idea of the dramatic things God was doing to prepare the spiritual ground for them.

One of the Hawaiian gods was Ku, the god of warfare. His priests demanded many human sacrifices, even as wars and skirmishes soaked the islands with blood. Their religion included the brutal *kapu* system, in which minor infractions, such as a woman eating a banana, were punishable by death.

After King Kamehameha I died, his favorite wife, Ka'ahumanu; the "sacred wife," Keopuolani; the high priest, Hewahewa;

and the new king, Kamehameha II, decided to abandon the Hawaiian religion and its cruel *kapu* laws.

Although they did away with the old religion, tearing down the *heiau* (temples) and demolishing the idols, they didn't replace the Hawaiian religion with anything. It was a remarkable, maybe unique, moment in history. As the little ship of missionaries sailed on their way, the Hawaiians created a spiritual vacuum waiting for something to fill it.

One of the Hawaiian priests also received a vision. He said the "new God" would come to their island "in a black box," with someone stepping onto a large rock on the shore of what is now called Kailua Kona.[2]

That's exactly what happened when the missionaries arrived in 1820 aboard the brig *Thaddeus*. The first to disembark stepped onto the big rock in Kailua Bay. He carried his Bible, protected from the elements in a small, black box.

What happened in the following years would have thrilled Henry Opukaha'ia. His people quickly embraced the new faith. Missionaries taught the people how to read, finished Henry's translation of Scripture, then used their press to print thousands of Hawaiian Bibles.

Within a short time, 90 percent of Hawaiians could read—the highest per capita literacy rate in the world at that time. Added to that, a census in 1853 showed that 96 percent were professing Christians. They received the work of the Holy Spirit in their lives and read the Bible in their mother tongue.

Hawai'i's Great Awakening

Following the spread of Bible knowledge, a great revival washed over the Hawaiian Islands in the 1830s and 1840s. It centered on the Big Island.

Titus Coan came with a new wave of missionaries. He'd experienced America's Second Great Awakening, having been converted at a revival meeting of Charles Finney.[3]

Based in Hilo, Coan evangelized tirelessly, preaching six to ten times a day, counseling seekers until midnight, then starting again at dawn. He maintained this pace for almost fifty years, marking off his parish in a radius of one hundred miles from the town. He taught the Bible in every household within that circle, to between fifteen and sixteen thousand people. Some homes hidden away in the mountains and valleys surrounding Hilo had no roads leading to them. Coan hacked his way through the jungle and climbed high, slippery paths to reach each one.[4]

He followed up with all those residents, keeping a "spiritual census" in his notebook. Who had died? Who had moved away and where were they now? Who had not yet received the message? Who had backslidden? Coan sought the latter repeatedly, calling them back to repentance. Who was following Christ faithfully? He made sure those received intensive training for months so they could join the church.

America's First Megachurch

Titus Coan's church soon became the largest in the world. When he died in 1882, he had added thirteen thousand members to his church in Hilo, plus many more through his evangelistic efforts on other islands.[5]

The Hawaiian church began to send out its own missionaries in the 1850s. Spiritual descendants of Henry Opukaha'ia took the gospel to the Marquesas Islands, to Micronesia, to the Gilbert Islands, and to parts of Melanesia.[6]

The story of Hawai'i demonstrates how ending Bible poverty can transform an entire country:

- The fervor of a spiritual awakening led to missionary vision.
- A young convert decided to return to his homeland to give them Jesus and the Bible, but he died suddenly.
- Others went to Hawai'i in his place. They gave the Bible to the people.
- The Hawaiians learned how to read, soon gaining the highest rate of literacy per capita in the world.
- A missionary named Titus Coan went to great effort to distribute God's Word to every home, including the most remote. His Bible teaching changed lives.
- The Spirit and the Word of God came together in Hawai'i's great awakening, with multitudes repenting and filling the churches.
- Hawaiians themselves became missionaries, going to far reaches of the Pacific.

"Jesus Speaks My Language!"

The Hawaiian example is being repeated all over the world today. The *ethnē*, or nations, are experiencing transformation.[7]

Morgan Jackson reports that when a people group, an *ethnos*, finally gets the Word of God in their own language, they often say, "Now we're a real people!"

Those who've never experienced the excitement of hearing Scripture in their native tongue for the first time don't understand. They ask, "Why can't they be satisfied to read a Bible in the majority language of their country? And why should we bother to translate into languages spoken only by a small group of people?"

When someone hears God's Word in their mother tongue, it touches them on a deep level. Perhaps it's because language is part of our identity. Like many before him, a tribesman receiving a recording of the Bible in his mother tongue marveled, "Jesus speaks my language!"

The founder of Wycliffe, William Cameron Townsend, said, "The greatest missionary is the Bible in the mother tongue. It needs no furlough and is never considered a foreigner."

It opens the people's hearts to the gospel. Christianity is no longer a foreigner's religion.

Not Understanding a Word in Church

In numerous parts of the world, most people in a minority language group cannot speak the majority language of their country, whether it's Hindi in India, Swahili in Kenya, or Pidgin English in Papua New Guinea.

One example is a church in Peru. The people gather every Sunday to hear their pastor preach in Spanish from a Spanish Bible. No one in the congregation understands a word. And they've been doing this for years.

While their devotion is commendable, often their behavior the rest of the week is not. Immorality and syncretism, the mixing of Christian belief with witchcraft, are pervasive in such situations.

How can you disciple people without a Bible? It's not just a problem in Peru. In many parts of the world warehouses are filled with Bibles and other Christian literature that the vast majority cannot read.

And what about the other objection? Is it a waste of time to translate the Bible into languages spoken by very few people?

The answer is in the words of Jesus. The Lord told us to go to "every," to reach "all" (Mark 16:15 KJV; Matt. 28:19–20). He didn't say to just reach the majority. John 3:16 doesn't say,

"For God so loved the majority." He loves the world. He doesn't want to leave anyone out.

Short-Term Volunteers Helping Linguists

For years I had been thinking of how we could get Bibles into languages faster. I thought of how I preach through interpreters in small crowds and large. I say a sentence, a concept, or a short paragraph, and then the translator tells them what I said.

I've asked why we couldn't do something similar to speed up Bible translation, producing verbally recorded Bibles. And I've discovered others, such as Faith Comes By Hearing, who had the same idea. They have been doing many thousands of verbal recordings for years.

It was a privilege to visit with Annette Jackson, wife of Jerry Jackson, founder of Faith Comes By Hearing. She told me story after story of their adventures reaching Bible-less peoples. She sometimes went on her own, climbing mountain trails in Papua New Guinea, living in remote villages, not coming back until she had another verbal recording of the Bible. She did language after language, forty in all, until she was in her mid-seventies. Now she's in her eighties and still finding ways to be part of ending Bible poverty.

When I meet people like the Jacksons, I feel that kindred spirit, trusting God for impossible things.

Verbal recordings of the Bible are more than a stopgap, a temporary measure. They are giving the Word of God to the people. Though it's best if people learn to read and have the Word of God in a text version, in the meantime they can have Bibles they can listen to.

The work of Bible translators will always be needed. They have been at the forefront of ending Bible poverty for one hundred years. They do a painstaking labor of love, taking years to learn a new language in the field with no one to teach them, identifying the grammar of that language, and sometimes devising written symbols.

We need both: those doing verbally recorded Bibles and the highly trained linguists who produce written copies of God's Word in the languages of the people. When missionaries give their verbally recorded Bibles to the translators, it helps the linguists produce quality, written translations much sooner. How wonderful to shorten the wait for written Bibles by years!

Jesus said to pray because "the laborers are few." In more than a half century of working with youthful short-term missionaries, we have seen that many of them decide to become long-term missionaries. This isn't just in YWAM but in virtually all missions. We often see young, short-term volunteers who help with verbal recordings of the Bible and new scripts of the *Jesus* film deciding to get training to become Bible linguists.

The overall work is speeding up. Missionaries are quickly creating verbal Bibles in new languages for hundreds of millions who can't read. People are downloading verbal Bibles from the internet and sharing them with one another on microSD cards. They can slip the Scriptures in their language into their mobile phones and handheld devices.

These are the ones from "every *ethnos*, tribe, people and language" (Rev. 7:9) who will be standing before the Lamb in white robes, waving palm branches.

They are gathering.

10

The Clock Is Racing

Christians are working on verbal recordings in a number of countries, including those of the vast "liquid continent," islands in the Pacific—Micronesia, Melanesia, and Polynesia. The region, also called Oceania or Pacifica, covers 32 million square miles, stretching from Hawai'i in the northeast to New Zealand and Papua New Guinea in the southwest.

Some of these islands are unimaginably remote. Some are so difficult to access that supply and mail boats come only three times a year, or even less frequently. For some, supply boats never come at all.

People on these faraway islands endure hardships. Because of limited food choices, many suffer from illnesses such as diabetes. They can fish, raise pigs, and cultivate taro and a few fruits and vegetables if conditions are right.

Education is spotty, and medical care is almost nonexistent. Unemployment is rampant. If given the opportunity, adult children immigrate to New Zealand, Australia, or the United States. They send part of their salaries back home to their families. Hopelessness plagues many.

However, nothing is too hard for God. He has plans for the islanders. We can't leave them isolated. And we can't leave them without Bibles in each language. Their development depends on it.

In Four Weeks, Eight New Languages

Oceania has the greatest linguistic diversity found anywhere in the world. Of its 1,121 languages, 426 lack any portion of the Bible. Of those 426 untargeted languages, 321 are in one country: Papua New Guinea (PNG).[1]

YWAM missionaries are working diligently to end Bible poverty in PNG. For example, some are assisting linguists and filmmakers to produce the *Jesus* film in new languages. Here's how that collaboration is working in PNG. First, Wycliffe does a translation of the Gospel of Luke in the target language. Then the people working with the *Jesus* film produce a script adaptation. The third step is where YWAMers come in. They have been trained to record a speaker of the mother tongue narrating the script. It's then dubbed for the movie.

A New Zealand couple, Bernie and Sylvia Kay, are part of our YWAM Kona family. They've been working in PNG to help the *Jesus* film people record new languages for the film. Recently their collaborative team hosted five students from a Discipleship Training School in Kona, Hawai'i. In four weeks' time, the students were able to help produce the narration of the *Jesus* film in eight new languages.

Five hundred thousand people speak those eight languages. Think of it! Half a million people are hearing and seeing the

Word of God in their own languages. And it only took four weeks for a handful of people to finish the process.

Verbal Bibles are an important way to help the 771 million on earth who cannot read.[2] And you can use local-to-local interpreters to produce them.[3]

The recorded Word of God is also popular with lots of people. Even though they know how to read, some prefer to gain information through audio or visual methods—audio when they're commuting, working out at the gym, gardening, or doing housework; films or videos when they're relaxing.

Boots on the Ground

The method of producing verbal interpretations of Bibles is spreading. Linguists are training lay volunteers to assist them in the translation process. Bible linguists are dedicated missionaries who are working to end Bible poverty. One of these groups, Wycliffe Bible Translators, has been serving the Lord by putting his Word into eager hands for decades and decades. Now they are asking for help. They can translate Bibles faster if they can get volunteers to be more "boots on the ground."

There are so many ways to be a part of Bible translation. You can locate speakers of minority languages to help create a verbal version of the Bible. You can assist with verbal recordings of the *Jesus* film in new languages. Logistical help is always needed to help translators, provide transportation or child care, or cook meals. You can spread the vision of ending Bible poverty in your church and community. Or you can gather friends to pray regularly for the distribution of the Word of God.

What Are We Waiting For?

Robin Green of Faith Comes By Hearing developed an app in partnership with Pioneer Bible Translators and the Seed Company. It's called Render. They designed it so that illiterate people can easily make verbal recordings of the Bible for their tribe.[4]

A local interpreter listens to the Bible in the majority language of his or her country and then creates a verbal recording in the mother tongue. Verbal recordings save local interpreters the work of learning to read, then creating an alphabet, then teaching literacy to the community, then writing down the translated Bible. It also saves an outsider from having to learn the new language, study its grammar, and create written symbols—all before they can begin translation. If they begin instead with verbal recordings, they can offer the people recorded Bibles quickly.

New technology and new methods are making digital recording and distribution easy. We can now reach the most isolated places. Considering all this, we must ask ourselves, what are we waiting for?

Why Did It Take You So Long?

A few years ago a leading missionary linguist said it would take 150 years to begin Bible translation for the last language without the Bible.

Now that date has been moved to 2025. I want to see it happen with verbal recordings even sooner—by December 25, 2020. I think we should also aim to have a written translation of the entire New Testament in every language by 2033. That year marks the two thousandth anniversary of Jesus giving us the Great Commission before he ascended into heaven.

We are privileged to be living in this time. We are going to see the fulfillment of dreams and visions. Although I would like to be alive to see it, I may not be. But I believe today's youth will experience the thrill of reaching everyone on the planet with the good news of Jesus Christ. Will we do our part, praying and taking steps of faith to see God's will carried out on earth as it is in heaven? Or will we delay what he wants to do through us?

I heard a story from Kenya recently. Missionaries had just completed the translation of the Bible for a tribe. As they passed out Bibles, the people rejoiced. All except for one man. He just stood there, holding the precious book in his hands. Finally he asked one of the foreigners, "Why did it take you so long to give us God's Word in our language?"

That's a good question. Why did it take us so long to take Bibles to everyone? And what about now? What are we waiting for?

11

Getting the Word Out

The Bible is powerful because God the Father authorizes it. It's powerful because Jesus is the Word within the Word, and because the Holy Spirit, who anointed its writing, speaks to us as we read or hear it. If we take up the challenge of ending Bible poverty, we will see its power.

We now have a variety of methods of producing digital and print copies of the Scriptures. During the Reformation they only had the printing press. I am amazed at how the people of that time maximized their one technological device.

One of my friends is Dr. Tom Bloomer, provost of the University of the Nations. He has lived in Switzerland for many years. Besides his academic studies, he likes to investigate historic sites in the area. It's been gratifying to take walks with Tom to some of these places.

One site is a small chapel next to the cathedral in Geneva. That was where John Calvin preached every Sunday. Someone always sat on a front bench to transcribe his sermons.

A side room off the chapel used to house one of Gutenberg's printing presses. As soon as Calvin finished a sermon, printers would take the transcript, set the type, and begin printing copies. The ink was barely dry when they gave these copies to riders, who would mount their horses and take the papers to the east, west, north, and south of Europe. Within one week, thousands of Europeans were reading Calvin's sermons.

If Western Europe could be transformed five hundred years ago with a printing press and fast horses, imagine what we can do now with the many innovations the Lord has given us. Other developments internationally have set the stage for us. As God's people have prayed, he has moved sovereignly to open doors. For instance, it seemed impossible that communist China would ever change. Who could have predicted how quickly it would open up to the world?

Deng Xiaoping Didn't Fear the Bible

In April 2014, I was in New Zealand talking with a missionary named Peter Dean. He was home on furlough from China. He reminded me that he used to be a printer in YWAM's castle in Hurlach, Germany.

Peter handed me a book. It was a Bible in Chinese. "Loren, we just printed the 100 millionth copy of the Bible in China. This is one from that printing."

I knew the story of the 100 million.

Deng Xiaoping was the de facto leader of China from the mid-1970s on. He wanted to set up a socialist market economy in China, so he invited a small group of Westerners to teach the Chinese about the free market system. The five businessmen he invited happened to be Christians.

After their talks ended, one of the men asked Deng through an interpreter, "Why are you communists afraid of the Bible?"

Deng threw back his head and laughed. "We don't fear the Bible! It's just a book."

"Then let us set up a printing press in China. Let us print one million Bibles for the Chinese people."

Deng laughed again. "One million in China is nothing. Go ahead!"

The businessmen went home and raised the money. Others came to do the printing, including Peter and another worker from Hurlach, Germany. They started printing in the very country into which we had previously smuggled many thousands of Bibles. Now Christians were printing them with Deng Xiaoping's approval. Chinese Christians were then able to distribute them.

When Peter and his coworkers finished printing one million Bibles, they did another million. And another million, and another, and another. From 1976 to 2014, they printed one million Bibles at a time, all with the approval of the late Deng Xiaoping.

And there in New Zealand, I was holding one of the 100 million.

Peter said they had just gotten new equipment and were now producing a Bible every four seconds!

"Google-berg"

Despite this striking change in China and the new super-fast printers, we could never print enough Bibles for everyone in the world. However, the Lord has allowed a solution for this time in history. The Reformers had the Gutenberg press. But, as David Hamilton says, now we have the "Google-berg." You could even call it the Google-berg Revolution.

Free Bibles can be downloaded from the internet. According to certain ministries, unnamed for security reasons, hundreds of thousands of Arabic speakers are downloading print and audio versions of God's Word.

Those without access to the internet can still get audio, video, animated, and text versions of the Bible. People in some of the most remote parts of the earth have mobile phones or tablets, even though they have no coverage. They use them to play music and movies.

As we've seen, once downloaded from the internet, apps can be shared from one person's handheld to another, possibly going viral. We can distribute SD or microSD cards with the Scriptures and the *Jesus* film in the local language. In restricted-access countries, we can set up mobile Wi-Fi hotspots, quietly offering free Bibles and the *Jesus* film to anyone nearby with a handheld.

Missionary Techies

Chong Ho is a dear friend of mine. He's a YWAM leader heading up a team of IT missionaries. Before joining YWAM he ran a private business as an Oracle database administrator. He consulted for the Department of Justice, the Department of Energy, and the Federal Aviation Administration. He also worked with several Fortune 500 companies, such as GE and IBM.

Now he's a missionary techie.

Chong Ho and I made several trips to South Korea in one year, speaking in large venues. We challenged anyone in the IT industry to help end Bible poverty by tithing their time, talent, and treasure. Giving 10 percent was not only for the CEOs. It was for their employees too. Companies could tithe the time and talent of their employees, as well as their treasure—a tenth of their profits. We asked them to create apps, devices, animated Bible stories, video games—anything God showed them to do.

The response throughout the IT industry of South Korea was immediate and significant.

On my fifth trip to Korea that year, Chong Ho and other IT specialists came along. We shared leadership in a phenomenal IT Missions Conference. More than one thousand people attended.

There we met with CEOs of companies. They had already begun to tithe those three things—their time, talent, and treasure. They showed us what they had created for ending Bible poverty.

Key leaders committed to do even more, including producing an animated version for each new translation of the Bible. As of the writing of this book, eighty CEOs of IT companies in Korea meet weekly for prayer, worship, and Bible study. They are working on projects to spread the Word of God.

Chong Ho and his team have recently made contact with Christians in Silicon Valley, in the Pacific Northwest, and in other places where leading US companies have their headquarters. He found that small Bible study and prayer groups were happening in every one of the IT giants. The YWAM techies visited and challenged several of those prayer groups to join the global cause of ending Bible poverty now.

The Internet, a Level Playing Field

Developers are working on ways to maximize God's Word on the internet. Some have been doing so for ten or twenty years. One of our other contacts, a Korean digital designer, has developed apps for networking and Bible distribution online. One of his products has become quite successful in South Korea and in many other countries.

These solutions are perfect for David-versus-Goliath situations. "The internet is a level playing field," says Chong Ho.

When I hear statements like that, I see endless opportunities.

I heard from three sources in the digital industry on America's West Coast. They were privy to the fact that leaders in the industry were aiming to give out four billion handhelds so that everyone on earth could access the internet by 2020. Unfortunately the project was shelved. No one could figure out how to make the solar-powered handhelds economically. And many millions without the internet don't have electricity either.

If the industry leaders had succeeded with solar-powered mobile phones it would have coordinated perfectly with the satellite project initiated by Elon Musk, one of the founders of Tesla.

Let's ask God to show someone how to create a handheld with built-in solar capability. It could be a Christian. Jesus has given his servants "downloads" of understanding before. Or he might even use a "Cyrus" to do his work.[1]

We *can* get a Bible into every home on earth. Some of these technological advances could be part of the answer. However, we must have the empowerment of the Holy Spirit above all. "'Not by might nor by power, but by my Spirit,' says the LORD Almighty" (Zech. 4:6).

12

Spreading Seeds

It's one of the most inspiring stories. A young Norwegian named Hans Nielsen Hauge listened to the Lord, then worked tirelessly to end Bible poverty in his country. He changed the course of history as he distributed Bibles throughout his nation.[1]

This happened at the beginning of the nineteenth century. Only the elite of the country had freedom. Most of the things God led Hauge to do were against the law, challenging the status quo.

Hans's parents were godly people and raised their son to fear the Lord. Although Hans was devout he wasn't sure of his personal salvation.

On a spring day in 1796 Hauge received what he called his "spiritual baptism." He was singing a hymn as he worked in his father's field. Abruptly he felt his heart lifted to God. In a rush of assurance, he knew Jesus had accepted him. His sins were forgiven! In that minute Hans also knew God was calling him to take his Word to everyone in Norway.

The situation in his country looked impossible. Norwegians were poor and starving. Sometimes famine seized the land, and many perished from hunger. They had only a few schools and no university. A bleak future lay ahead, with the people eking out a living in small farms and fishing villages.

Defying the Law, Obeying the Call

Norway's neighbors had subjugated them for hundreds of years. Denmark, their conqueror at that time, made it illegal for them to travel or meet publicly. What's more, only ministers of the state church were allowed to preach. Anywhere.

Despite all that, Hans had a calling from God. He defied the law and crisscrossed the country, preaching and distributing Bibles. Within eight years his ministry spread God's Word throughout Norway. To do this, he covered fifteen thousand kilometers (more than nine thousand miles) on foot or on skis.[2]

Hans learned that the Bible was a great source of practical education for himself and for working people. He wrote book after book giving biblically based advice on many topics, including farming, educating children, creating new wealth by doing honest commerce, and of course becoming a disciple of the Lord Jesus Christ. He became a best-selling author with two hundred thousand copies in print—remarkable in a country of only nine hundred thousand!

He also created thirty businesses in various towns.[3] At one site alone he built a paper mill, a stamping mill, a bone mill, a flour mill, a tannery, and a foundry. He helped his followers find job opportunities in other towns too. In these ways he transformed the economy of the entire country.

Hans could have become a wealthy man because of the many businesses he launched and the popularity of the books he wrote. But time after time he gave away his money to help others.[4]

The vast majority of Norwegians were illiterate. But they wanted to read the Bible and Hauge's many books. This created a demand for schools to teach them how to read and write. The literacy rate began to climb.

Languishing in Chains

Despite all these positive changes, the government and religious authorities were outraged. So were the upper classes. They resented the lower classes for not staying in their "place." But Hauge and his followers continued, even though he was imprisoned fourteen times in seven years.[5]

He formed one thousand home groups, which cooperated with the state church. These groups prayed and studied the Bible together, holding one another accountable for behavior contrary to Scripture. They dared to travel, meeting with other Hauge groups.

Hauge's biblical teaching influenced all spheres. Leaders emerged, eventually becoming politically active. Families were strengthened and businesses flourished, helping to create a middle class. The common people learned to read and then, encouraged by Hauge, explored all sorts of books.

The church came alive.

Even though the fruit of his ministry became apparent, Hans still languished in chains. His last imprisonment lasted nearly ten years, and when he was released, his health was broken. He died when he was only fifty-two.

He didn't live long enough to see the full impact of his ministry. He simply obeyed Jesus' command in Matthew 28:19–20,

throwing his whole self into distributing and eventually publishing Bibles as well as educating his followers in how the Word
of God applies to every area of life. His small groups helped one
another and the churches to engage with Scripture on a daily
basis. And they bathed all their efforts in prayer.

Hauge's work played a major part in creating a free Norway.
After his death, three of his followers were part of the group
who created the first constitution.

His life also shows that we may pay a high price to end Bible
poverty. But we will bring eternal reward to millions of people.

13

Ships, Partner Ships, and a Big Canoe

When it comes to ending Bible poverty, I believe the hardest places won't be countries ruled by vicious dictators or areas where they are killing Christians. Nor will it be reaching tribes in the dense jungles of the Amazon, the remote villages in the Himalayas, or the nomadic tribes of the Sahara.

The most difficult will be the islands of the Pacific. Jesus said, "Go into the uttermost part of the earth." From Jerusalem, where Jesus spoke those words, Oceania is literally halfway around the earth. The "uttermost part." It's difficult to evangelize there but not because they're hostile to the message. Most islanders welcome missionaries. But as we saw in chapter 10, the challenges in reaching these far-flung places are enormous.

Let's look at the facts for Micronesia, Melanesia, and Polynesia:

- Sprinkled over the largest ocean on earth are 1,072 inhabited islands and atolls.
- Only 64 of the 1,072 islands have an adequate port for boats and ships.
- Airports and airstrips are also hard to find, located only on 215 islands.[1]

Some of the islands of Melanesia are nine hundred miles from an airport. Pitcairn is one of the most remote. My family and I sailed there with others on YWAM's ship, the *Pacific Ruby*, for ministry in 1991. Pitcairners are descendants of the mutineers from the *Bounty*, plus women they picked up in Tahiti. The island sits far from everyone in the southeastern edge of the Pacific. It can take a ten-day voyage to get someone to a hospital. If a resident of Pitcairn has an appendicitis attack, it is likely a death sentence.

The isolation of these islands requires carefully planned Bible distribution. Fortunately, the Lord has sparked a major renewal of the ship vision within YWAM. We now have twenty-four ships available, most of them smaller vessels. They are ideal for accessing dots of land surrounded by hidden reefs. When the ships reach the islands, they focus on YWAM's threefold ministry—evangelism, training, and acts of mercy.

In addition to these, we have "Partner Ships," a program in which owners lend their crafts for missionary efforts. In early January 2015, in a storm off the Kona Coast, we lost a sailing ship and one precious YWAMer, Aaron Bremner. The tragedy touched people's hearts, and some families gave their ships to replace the *Hawai'i Aloha*.

That's why we're calling our effort to place a Bible in every home of Micronesia "Project Aaron." We want to honor him and his commitment to the Lord and to the islands of the Pacific.

Lib Island

Some of those ships are already engaged in ending Bible poverty in Melanesia, in the hinterlands of Papua New Guinea, and in Micronesia. Smaller vessels with a shallower draft—needing less water depth—are the only way to get teams ashore on islands with neither an airstrip nor a port.

YWAM Ships Captain Ann Ford tells about Lib Island, one of the Marshall Islands on which they were unable to drop anchor. The island has a narrow, submerged shelf around it. Next to that ring there is a sheer drop-off where the water turns dark blue. Residents don't even know its depth. Beyond the deep, circling it, is coral reef.

Islanders blasted a hole through the reef so that small motorboats could enter. As the YWAM ship bobbed on open seas, Captain Ann and some of the crew climbed down from the vessel into small boats manned by the islanders. They were shuttled to the island, shooting through the hole in the reef, crossing the deep blue water, and finally reaching the shore.

Lib Island is like almost all the far-flung islands. There are no doctors and no dentists. They hadn't had any visitors for ten years. During that time, many of the population had died. That's why YWAM Ships' first attraction is often the medical help they bring. Teams include doctors, dentists, and nurses from various countries doing short-term or long-term mission work. Like all YWAM missionaries, the medical volunteers pay their own way to come.

While the doctors, nurses, and dentists treat the people, the rest of the team gives basic health care training. They also lead people to Christ and give them verbal and printed Bibles in their language.

Like their isolated counterparts in the Himalayas, many of the islanders have smartphones and tablets, even though they have no internet access. They use them to store and trade movies and music.

YWAM Ships is able to use the LightStream technology I mentioned earlier. It creates a Wi-Fi hotspot that relays media in areas with no internet access. Islanders seeking medical care come onto the ship. While they wait to be seen by a doctor, they can use their mobile phones to watch and download gospel media via LightStream. Teams also take the LightStream devices into villages when they go ashore for evangelism, teaching, medical services, and sports.

Think of a Big Canoe

Earlier I shared how unprecedented unity among the body of Christ is paving the way for an end to Bible poverty. Several mission groups have entered into a committed partnership in the Pacific. They've named it *Wa'a* (pronounced Va-a), the Polynesian word for "canoe." The mission groups in Wa'a include Wycliffe Global Alliance, SIL, Jesus Film Project, Seed Company, Cru, Faith Comes by Hearing, Island Breeze, and YWAM—especially 4K Mapping, University of the Nations, and YWAM Ships. Other organizations have also joined in on various regional meetings.

Why did they call their partnership "canoe"?

Thousands of years ago Polynesians crossed the largest ocean in the world in canoes, setting their course by the stars. To do so, they had to commit themselves to the task, relying on one another's strength, paddling in harmony and perfect rhythm.

That's how this partnership among the mission groups is working. Wa'a began when Wycliffe approached YWAM. Wycliffe and its alliance members send out highly trained, disciplined, godly people. SIL, one of its alliance members, has the largest number of working linguists in the world. They have the expertise, but they need more help. As we've seen, translation can be done faster with the help of short-term volunteers with a bit of training.

We felt the Lord wanted YWAM to recruit short-term helpers. Wa'a fit with the vision God had already given us, to end Bible poverty.

Shouting over the Waves

After dedicating ourselves to taking God's Word all over the Pacific, some of our participants decided to walk down to the Kona seashore to pray. The group stopped at the water's edge, facing the Pacific Ocean. There they arranged themselves into the outline of a canoe. They began to pray, shouting over the crashing waves, giving themselves afresh to Jesus and to the Wa'a vision. They were loving and obeying God with their strength as well as their heart, mind, and soul.

Wa'a is similar to the Table 71 group—both have drawn together people from different missions, collaborating on finishing the Great Commission. Like Table 71, Wa'a members share data and progress with one another, avoiding duplication of efforts. Member organizations show mutual honor and respect while keeping their unique identities and ministry focus.

This mirrors the honor that islanders and visitors show one another. Like the ancient paddlers of canoes, Wa'a team members work in harmony, putting their backs into it, depending on one another's strengths.

It has only been a handful of years since Wa'a began, yet they are already seeing results.

"That's why young people are getting excited," says Ben Nonoa, a New Zealander of Samoan descent. "I'm trusting we'll see waves of islanders going out as missionaries again, responding as they did in 1839." He was referring to the first Samoan missionaries. Nine years after they first met the Lord, they sailed to Vanuatu, the Solomons, northern Australia, and Papua New Guinea. Some were martyred, even cannibalized, but more took their place.

Like the Ark of the Covenant

Vae Eli is a Samoan of royal blood and a YWAMer. He was a missionary for thirty years in Europe, Asia, the Pacific, and North America. But Vae says he was unaware of the severe Bible poverty in his home region. Then he heard about one of those countries, Vanuatu, that has eleven languages without the Word of God. The Solomon Islands have fourteen Bible-less languages. Vae says these people groups are like his cousins, yet he didn't know of their need.

Then it hit Vae. Samoa used to be without God's Word too. The missionaries made an alphabet and a writing system, and they translated the Scriptures for Vae's ancestors. He wouldn't be able to read the Bible in Samoan if they hadn't come! They didn't merely give his forefathers the greatest book in the world. The missionaries taught them how to read. Now Vae could know his own story. All Samoans could. They could preserve their culture and identity as a people.

Vae wept for days after he realized this. He and his wife, Julie, left their ministry among First Nations tribes in Canada. They returned to the Pacific to help end Bible poverty.

Vae says most of us don't understand the importance of the Bible. That understanding struck him when he visited a village in Vanuatu where the locals were receiving their first copies of God's Word. Hundreds came to celebrate. Chiefs and warriors decked themselves out in feathers and in jewelry made of shells, seeds, and bits of bone. They chanted and danced for joy. Then while they sang, young warriors bore the precious book in a box, perched on poles they carried on their shoulders—like it was the Ark of the Covenant. God was coming to live among them and speak from his book.

Having Scripture in your own language is a truly priceless treasure. As Vae said, Bible translation is about more than finishing a project. It's God saying to the people, "I'm available to you. I speak your language."

14

The Gift of Understanding

We need to end Bible poverty—in our world, our nations, our communities, our families, and ourselves.

Yes. In ourselves.

We can own a bookshelf full of Bibles. We can access many translations of God's Word on our smartphones. We can have world-class Bible teachers available to us on YouTube or elsewhere on the internet. With a few clicks we can open commentaries for insights into the original Hebrew and Greek. But if we aren't also making devotional time for God's Word, if we aren't asking the Holy Spirit to speak to us, or if we're merely reading from a sense of duty or a careless attitude, we can develop Bible poverty ourselves.

We've already seen how Bible ignorance is growing, even among those who go to church every Sunday. Modern culture educates people all week through film, the internet, celebrity interviews, political speeches, the school system, the business culture, news commentators . . . The list goes on and on. How then can we expect a twenty-minute sermon once a week to help us understand the Bible, especially when popular culture is contradicting it 24/7?

A recent Barna survey revealed a growing rejection of faith among Americans. The percentage of adults who say the Bible is not a holy book has doubled in the past six years. Millennials are the most skeptical, with 22 percent saying the Bible is not sacred.[1] What are we to do about this?

Falling in Love with the Lord and His Word

The psalmist tells us how to stand firm in a society that is turning from the Lord. In the first two verses of Psalm 1, he says we should not walk in step nor take a stand with the skeptics. We shouldn't sit with mockers. And we should never sit in silence while they malign the character of God. Instead, we should delight in God's Word, thinking carefully and prayerfully about it day and night.

We will make time for whatever we find delightful. As we immerse ourselves in Scripture, relying on the Spirit to bring fresh revelation, we will find ourselves delighting more and more in God's Word. The result is that we will grow to love him more and more. This is also how we begin to change our world. It seems obvious, doesn't it? We can't share what we don't have. We can't see our culture transformed if we aren't continually being transformed ourselves.

It's especially important to study those parts of the Bible that teach principles relating to the most important parts of community life. Because these are the ones under attack from the enemy.

Seven Classrooms

During a family vacation on the western slope of the Rockies in Colorado, I was seeking the Lord, asking him how we could obey what Jesus commanded in Matthew 28:19–20. The year was 1975. Even then the United States was turning away from biblical principles with alarming speed. So were other nations.

I prayed, "Lord, how can we teach a nation?" We were supposed to be making disciples. But how could we do so when so many were tearing down the foundations?

Then the Lord gave me an idea. *There are seven classrooms, the most effective ways to influence a community or a nation.* I'd never heard of this concept, but I grabbed a yellow legal pad and pen and wrote as fast as I could.

The first "classroom" was the family; second, education; third, government; fourth, public communication; fifth, what we now call "celebration"—arts, entertainment, and sports; sixth, economy, which includes science, technology, medical, and business; and seventh, religious institutions.

Later we would see how the Bible is filled with these seven, with wisdom and instruction for each category. We would also later call them "spheres" instead of "classrooms." But on that summer day in 1975, I knew the seven were about training, making disciples of the nations.

As I finished my list, a forest ranger came up to our cabin. "You have a call at the ranger station, Mr. Cunningham. It's seven miles away." When I got to the station, I found the phone call was from an assistant of Bill Bright's. Bill was the founder of Campus Crusade for Christ (Cru). He wanted to invite Darlene and me to meet with him and his wife, Vonette, the next day in Boulder.

So we flew over the mountains. When we arrived I was glad I had grabbed my blue blazer. I knew Bill always wore one. He never appeared in public without a tie, either.

As we greeted one another, I reached into my jacket to pull out my yellow piece of paper. The list of seven. But before I could get mine unfolded, Bill had a piece of white paper out.

"Loren, look what the Lord just gave me!"

I looked at his list in wonder. It was worded a bit differently, but he had the same items and the same idea. This was the way God wanted us to influence every country.

Three weeks later, Darlene happened to see Dr. Francis Schaeffer on television. He was talking about the same seven elements of any country.

Since then the idea of the seven has spread to others in the body of Christ. Some call it "The Seven Mountains." It's obvious the Lord wants his people to understand this concept again at this point in history.[2]

Hans Nielsen Hauge also understood this. He proved the Bible has answers for every area of life. That idea changed Norway dramatically. As members of Hauge's small groups discovered, literacy, leadership, and knowledge increased at the same pace as their understanding of the Bible.

Our lives and our nations will be blessed when we become disciples and make disciples in the seven spheres.

The Bible Is Not Enough

Yes, the Bible has the answers. But we also need the Holy Spirit to guide us into Scripture. We need him to give us revelation. It goes beyond training or education. We need to hear his voice as we read. Has a Scripture ever stood out to capture your attention as you read? That's often how the Holy Spirit applies the Word to your heart.

The Scriptures were written by "prophets, [who] though human, spoke from God as they were carried along by the Holy

Spirit" (2 Pet. 1:21). Second Timothy 3:16 says, "All Scripture is God-breathed and is useful for teaching, rebuking, correcting and training in righteousness." That's the way people wrote the Bible. They were carried along by the Holy Spirit and God breathed his Word through them. In a similar way we need the Spirit to carry us along when we read his Word. We need the breath of God to understand it and apply it.

The other side of the coin is also true. If we do not rely on the Spirit when we read God's Word, we can misunderstand it, or even become deceived. The Scriptures warn that "the letter kills, but the Spirit gives life" (2 Cor. 3:6). Bible study is good. But if you separate it from dependence on the Holy Spirit, the result can be cold, hard legalism. This is why we must study his Word in an attitude of prayer.

15

Training Outside the Box

We also need the Lord's guidance when we train others. Otherwise we will rely on our own education, teaching the way our teachers taught us. We will miss the ways the Lord wants to use us in these rapidly changing times. We want to teach timeless truths in innovative ways. Only the Lord can keep us on the cutting edge. He is never caught by surprise.

Leaning on him for revelation rather than trusting old habits is vital when we're training cross-culturally. The Holy Spirit never has culture shock either. He knows every culture of every *ethnē* on the planet intimately. He will give us the right approach for our students.

When the Lord led us to found the University of the Nations, we had to depend on the Holy Spirit's guidance. We were beginning a university unlike any other. It was clearly time for a new wineskin for new wine (Matt. 9:17).

Something Unlike Anything Else

The Lord graciously guided us in our foundational years. He blessed our efforts and then gave us bigger challenges, stretching us more and more. Some of what he taught us may help as you step into your calling.

During those beginning years of the university, the Lord was calling us to do something none of us had experienced or learned in our academic backgrounds. We asked him for the details. How do we organize our courses? What spiritual and academic requirements do we set? How do we keep Jesus at the center of every course, not just the religious ones?

There isn't space to tell all the unique characteristics the Lord told us to put into the University of the Nations.[1] But I'll share one bit of guidance he gave us for the Discipleship Training School (DTS).

The Lord called our attention to 2 Peter 1:5, where the apostle told his converts, "Add to your faith virtue; and to virtue knowledge" (KJV). We noticed the order in which Peter placed those values. First, our students should have faith—choosing to believe God, to hear and obey his Word. Next, they were to add virtue—they must stay true to Jesus, growing to be more like him. Finally, they would be ready to gain knowledge.

Take our entry point for instance, the DTS. When someone wants to enroll in the University of the Nations or work with us on staff, he or she first attends a DTS.

We currently operate almost two thousand DTSs in seven hundred locations in 160 nations, teaching our students in about one hundred languages. During the school, students learn to know God better and make him known to others. They find out how to hear the voice of God by submitting to the Holy Spirit and listening to him. As they take steps of obedience, they discover the faithfulness of God to provide for their needs and open doors for them.

The First Temptation

It's a mistake to begin with knowledge instead of faith and virtue. That was the original temptation in the Garden of Eden. The serpent offered them knowledge so they could "be like God" (Gen 3:5). People often say knowledge is power. But if we gain knowledge without faith and virtue, we might end up wielding that power in an unrighteous way.

The order of those qualities in 2 Peter 1:5 is why we require our U of N students to complete the DTS first. After that we offer courses that add knowledge to faith and virtue. We have more than five hundred upper-level schools, seminars, and workshops offering training in the seven spheres. But it all begins with faith and virtue.

Stepping into the Bible

While every U of N course is founded on God's Word, some focus entirely on the Bible. There are plenty of fascinating courses, but I'll tell about two that offer new ways to encounter God's Word.

In the School of Biblical Studies (SBS), students read through the entire Bible, outlining it chronologically, studying every verse of Scripture five times, writing thirteen hundred sermon outlines, and drawing a chart of the entire Bible. While completing such training is a significant achievement, what's more important is the process of *baptizo*—soaking in the Word. These SBS courses are offered in forty countries.

Another school, Word by Heart, is a different way to experience Scripture. Think of it as Bible training combined with a school of drama. Instead of learning by repetition, the students step into the story. They memorize an entire Gospel, such as Luke, presenting it as a dramatic, word-for-word, one-person play. Word by Heart schools are now scattered over six continents.

When I first heard a Word by Heart presentation, I felt like I was on the streets of Jerusalem two thousand years ago, encountering Jesus along with his original audience.

From Culture to Culture and Sphere to Sphere

Of course, we are not the only ones helping to end Bible poverty through education. Jesus taught his followers concepts that turned their lives upside down. The church has engaged in training from its beginning.

In our time, special ministries have offered biblical training to various segments of society. One of the best is the Alpha Course. It's designed for non-churchgoers and new Christians as "a practical introduction to the Christian faith."[2] A host couple invites people to come for dinner. They tell their guests ahead of time that their questions about Christianity will be answered. Because the approach is warm and friendly, Alpha Course has led to countless conversions and church growth.

Tens of thousands of Alpha Courses are running in 110 countries. It's quickly spreading to prisons, businesses, and schools; in the United States, Alpha is offered in more than two thousand churches and in more than forty-eight denominations, from Roman Catholic to Pentecostal.[3] In the UK, where Alpha began, it has reached 1.5 million Brits.

Of course, Bible study differs from culture to culture and sphere to sphere. When we speak of an end to Bible poverty through education, we include everyone. Significant differences exist: cultural, urban versus rural settings, belief systems before learning of Christ, and of course, language. Some people groups have had the Bible in their language for centuries. Others have only recently received one. That's why we must each ask the Lord how to accomplish the calling he's giving us.

To end Bible poverty we need the whole body of Christ. No matter which of the seven spheres you connect with most, there is something you can do. What experience, talents, or gifts has the Lord given you? Ask him what part he wants you to play. There are numerous possibilities.

Becoming Literate at Stunning Speed

This story may sound unbelievable, but I saw it happen. It's a miracle of a different kind.

Some of our staff, including David Hamilton, a longtime YWAM leader and international vice president for Strategic Innovation at the University of the Nations, had been studying the problem of the hundreds of millions who couldn't read. This meant they couldn't read the Bible or study the commentaries of men and women of God. They couldn't use the internet or record their own history. Above all, they couldn't develop their God-given talents. This kept them in poverty. They felt inferior.

David's group had been meeting to research and pray about this for six years. They knew the problem of worldwide illiteracy, they just couldn't come up with the answer.

A few years ago, during a leadership meeting in Kona, we were waiting on the Lord.

As we sat praying in silence, I thought of what David had been struggling with. I felt led to go over and lay my hands on his head. Others joined me as we asked the Lord to use him in a new and powerful way. We asked God to give David a creative word.

The moment we prayed, God gave David a "download." It was a new writing system. It rushed into his mind, the whole plan, how it would work, and the way it would apply to every language.

A Linguistic Game Changer

Soon David began working with others on this system. Edson and Marcia dos Santos Suzuki were part of the group. They are veteran linguists who decoded languages of indigenous tribes in the Amazon for more than twenty years. They began to develop the system the Lord had given to David.

They named it UniSkript.[4] It is the first system that can reduce all seven thousand spoken, written, and unwritten languages of the world into a usable orthography. Orthography is "the representation of the sounds of a language by written or printed symbols."[5]

UniSkript is a game changer in the world of linguistics. No written language in history has used characters that show how to use the lips, palate, mouth, and throat to make the sounds of speech.[6] UniSkript does this. People look at the symbols and know immediately how to sound it out. As they pronounce the symbols, they recognize one of their words. They go on to the next symbols and say another word. Soon they are reading their language. It's intuitive. We describe it as "icono-phono-logical." The symbols are "icons," showing where the sounds are made in the physical body. "Phono" shows how the sounds are made. Also it's "logical." It makes sense. People instantly recognized it.

Universities are now discovering UniSkript, the innovation God gave in an instant. We have eighty-four patents on UniSkript. The patent lawyer said he has never handled something so amazing. He said, "This will do more good than all the religions in the world put together!"

I'm not sure about his assessment, but UniSkript has been tested on six continents with more than thirty languages. The tests revealed those using UniSkript can teach people to read in their mother tongue in two weeks or less.

Many recognize how revolutionary it is. But we know God provided UniSkript to end illiteracy and Bible poverty, and to finish the Great Commission.

16

Engaging with the Word

Before we can see transformation in our communities, in our cities, or in our countries, we have to be transformed ourselves. It starts with us.

The Bible is not just a book or an app. It's the Lord Jesus opening his heart to us, welcoming us as a friend. It's there that we encounter the living God. As we open our Bibles and our hearts to the Holy Spirit, we begin to change. Saint Paul compared the Bible to bathing: "Christ loved the church and gave himself up for her to make her holy, cleansing her by the washing with water through the word" (Eph. 5:25–26).

We can also think of the Bible as a *Star Wars* lightsaber, slashing away things that don't belong. "For the word of God is alive and powerful. It is sharper than the sharpest two-edged sword, cutting between soul and spirit, between joint and marrow. It exposes our innermost thoughts and desires" (Heb. 4:12 NLT).

When we open our hearts and minds to God's Word, we become new people. We learn to know him and become his friends. We don't want to bring pain to his heart. That's the real motivation for change. When Potiphar's wife tried to trap Joseph into a sexual liaison, Joseph wasn't worried about losing his position or his reputation. He was alarmed at the thought of sinning against God because he was his friend (Gen. 39:9).

That's where transformation begins. It's as if your mind becomes rewired. Instead of living for yourself, you live for the Lord. Paul describes the process: "Do not conform to the pattern of this world, but be transformed by the renewing of your mind. Then you will be able to test and approve what God's will is—his good, pleasing and perfect will" (Rom. 12:2).

Detoxing the Mind

Danny Lehmann, a close friend, has been a missionary with YWAM since 1980. He used to surf and hang out on California beaches. Like multitudes of young people in the 1970s, he damaged his mind and body with drugs.

One day Danny was surfing at Hook Beach in Santa Cruz. Two young men walked up to him on the beach and gave him a gospel tract. After he was alone, he read it and gave his life to Jesus. He was thrilled to know he was right with God and on the way to his new life. There was one problem, though. He knew his soul was saved, but his mind and body were still messed up from all the drugs.

Danny plunged into the Word of God every day. He started memorizing key portions. The more he read and memorized, the more he wanted. He says the Bible was washing his brain, clearing his thinking, and restoring his memory. His long-term drug habit lost its appeal, and he stopped getting drunk. As he continued to memorize passages, his mind began to heal and his body grew strong. He was being transformed.

Danny is now a zealous evangelist and a charismatic leader, motivating and training thousands of young people internationally every year. He serves as the dean of the College of Christian Ministries at the University of the Nations. And he still has that gospel tract two young men gave him on the beach years ago.

Former US attorney general John Ashcroft is an acquaintance of mine. His father encouraged me during some difficult days not long after we began Youth With A Mission.

Recently Ashcroft said, "If we put the Word of God into the mouths of people, it will find its way to the hearts of people. Once it's in their hearts, it finds its way into the hands and feet."[1] As transformation happens in person after person, finding its way from their hearts into their hands and feet, a spiritual awakening begins to stir. Energy mounts. It's like the power that pushes a giant wave. The water isn't what causes it to crash on shore. It's the energy pushing the water forward.

The Holy Spirit is the one who's providing the energy, pushing the waves. God's Word says it's "not by might nor by power, but by my Spirit" (Zech. 4:6). We can't push the waves, but we can ride them. Soon the waves will flood the whole world, like in the vision Habakkuk saw (Hab. 2:14).

Experiencing the Drama of God's Story

We've seen how God has stirred people to create innovations that help us in this great push. Because of technology, God has made it easier and faster to take his Word to the whole world.

Other innovations allow us to experience the Bible in new ways. The SourceView suite of Bibles is designed for students of God's Word. It's also for youth and adults. These Bibles open up new ways of experiencing God's Word.

The first in the suite, SourceView, uses colors and layout to indicate who is speaking. Some say it's like reading a movie script. The story comes front and center. Red shows when one of the Trinity is speaking. Black denotes the narrator of the book, while green is used for primary characters, and blue for everyone else.

SourceView is ideal for small Bible study groups and family devotions. Members can pick one of the colors, then take turns reading the Scripture aloud. When an individual is studying God's Word alone, he or she can easily track who is speaking and what is going on—almost as if reliving what happened thousands of years ago.

It's the first major change in text formatting since the Scriptures were broken into verses more than five hundred years ago.[2]

A Billion Ways to Study and Understand the Bible

The second in the suite is the SphereView Bible. It's an unprecedented aid for Bible study. Because it's such an innovation, it's hard to describe. It would be impossible to put into a book. In fact it's not a book at all. It's an app. The IT revolution had to come to the point it is right now before it could have been done.

As you can tell by its name, this app for studying the Bible shows the seven spheres throughout the verses of the Old and New Testaments. It has icons and color-coding that show which of the seven spheres each verse relates to. Since many verses relate to two or more spheres, this requires a digital format. Think of it as each verse wrapped in layers of meaning, with a multitude of links you can follow to other passages.

With a few clicks, you can access every Scripture relating to a certain sphere, or a sphere as it relates to a people group, like Israel. Or you can explore one sphere's relation to another sphere. You may want to know everything Jesus said about family concerns, or when he said it. You can then search for what the Bible says about the family relating to government.

It's dazzling. With all its metadata, the SphereView offers more than a billion and a half ways to explore God's Word.

The two others in the suite are VerbView Bible and CommandView. They will be released soon after the publishing of this book and will also be digital. VerbView reveals the character of God, showing in each verse what he has thought and felt, the words he has spoken, and the actions he has taken. The CommandView displays everything God expects of human beings. It shows how each command is motivated by Father God's heart of love for us.

All four in the digital suite of Bibles will connect. So you will be able to see, for example, everything God said he will do for families who follow his commands. These are some of the awesome gifts the Lord has given us for this time in history. We are blessed to see these things.

17

A Dangerous Book

Have you wondered why tyrants fear the Bible? They pretend it's a book of fairy tales, telling about a God who doesn't exist. If so, why do they destroy every Bible they find? Why do they imprison or kill people who have a Bible or believe in the God of the Bible? What do they fear? And why do people risk their lives for a copy?

The Bible is dangerous to those who want to exercise absolute control. Jesus said, "If you hold to my teaching, you are really my disciples. Then you will know the truth, and the truth will set you free" (John 8:31–32).

Horace Greeley was a great journalist and an activist against slavery. He ran for US president in the nineteenth century. Greeley famously said, "It is impossible to enslave, mentally or socially, a Bible-reading people. The principles of the Bible are the groundwork of human freedom."

The Word of God sets people free politically. But it also brings freedom in other ways. As we saw in Danny Lehmann's story, it sets the mind and body free. It liberates people from personal sin, as it did for the tribe in Guatemala mentioned in chapter three. Church members there found freedom from alcoholism, domestic violence, and adultery after they read the Bible in their own language. The Bible sets people free from ignorance and cultural bondage, as experienced in Norway by Hans Nielsen Hauge's groups. The Word of God also enables people to transform the spheres to which they've been called.

What Happened to the Murder Capital?

A few years ago I met with Ed Silvosa of Argentina. Ed said he wanted to tell me about Juárez, Mexico. I knew the area well. YWAM has a beautiful location outside Juárez called Rancho de los Amigos. It is a ministry for orphans.

I also knew the terrible reputation of Juárez and the state of Chihuahua. Until recently, the area was one of the deadliest places in the world. Drug cartels waged war against one another and against the townspeople—men, women, and children. They killed tens of thousands in a handful of years.

Mayors and police officers were the biggest targets. Some were beheaded, others beaten to death. Gangs murdered eleven mayors in the area in 2010.[1] The carnage was horrific.

When the Silvosas visited Juárez, Ed asked the residents to pray for their police and their streets. They began to intercede. The crime rate plummeted. After a few years passed, people took notice. According to a CNN report, more than three thousand people had been killed in 2011. But as of April, only eighty-nine had died in 2015.[2]

"Look at this, Loren." Ed held out a photo. I looked and saw the skyline of the city. A sign on a mountainside facing the city read "Ciudad Juárez." Then I noticed. Below the sign, residents had used white rocks to spell out "La Biblia es Verdad. Lea La." It meant, "The Bible Is Truth. Read It."

The writer of the CNN report quoted several sources who ventured theories about why the crime rate had dropped. They didn't have a real answer. But we know. Juárez shows that prayer and the Bible are the only means for transformation.

A Worn-Out Bible

Listen to what one Christian leader says about his much-used Bible: "If you could see my Bible, you would not be particularly impressed. . . . Such an old, worn-out book! [But] I love my old Bible, which has accompanied me half my life. It has been with me in my times of joy and times of tears. It is my most precious treasure—I live out of it, and I wouldn't take anything in the world for it."

Those are the words of Pope Francis. That might surprise some. But when my wife and I, along with three other YWAM-ers, had a private meeting with the pontiff in November 2014, we found a man who loves Jesus and loves the Bible.

In an article from the Catholic News Agency, Pope Francis called the Bible a "highly dangerous book." He said, "There are more persecuted Christians in the world today than in the early days of the Church." Believers are often persecuted because they wear a cross or have a Bible.

Pope Francis also shared his own Bible reading habits. "Often I read a little and then put it away and contemplate the Lord. Not that I see the Lord, but he looks at me. He's there. I let myself look at him. And I feel—this is not sentimentality— I feel deeply the things that the Lord tells me. Sometimes he does not speak. I then feel nothing, only emptiness, emptiness,

emptiness. . . . But I remain patiently, and so I wait, reading and praying."

The pope said he sometimes falls asleep while praying. "But it does not matter. I'm like a son with the father, and that is what's important."

Recently, Pope Francis urged one million young people at a youth gathering in Poland to engage with the Bible every day. He said the Bible isn't meant to be on our shelves but in our hands. "Ask yourself if God is touching you in the depths of your longing," he said. "Only in this way can the force of the Word of God unfold. Only in this way can it change our lives, making them great and beautiful."[3]

18

It's Not a Suggestion

Is it possible to end Bible poverty all over the world? It is if we all do our part. No one organization or movement has the resources to finish Bible translation, production, and distribution. Our resources are like the five small barley loaves and two fishes. We must see what is already in our hands. Everyone has something. We need to pray, give financially, and go—whether next door or to the remotest islands, jungles, and mountain villages in the world.

It's going to happen. The Lord is pressing us into action. He has given us talented people and anointed partnerships. He has led men and women to create amazing technological tools. But we need to give him our loaves and fishes before he can multiply them.

One Million Intercessors

Our first step is prayer. Our enemy is more powerful than mere humans, but he will not prevail over the Holy Spirit and the prayers of intercessors. As 1 John 4:4 says, "The one who is in you is greater than the one who is in the world."

I'm calling for one million commitments from those who will petition the Lord regularly until this vision is fulfilled. A dear friend and a leader in the global prayer movement, Mike Bickle, is also seeking one million to pray daily to end Bible poverty and complete the Great Commission.

Are you willing to pray? If so, go to EndBiblePovertyNow.com and sign the pledge.

Besides prayer, there are other ways to get involved. You can go on a short-term mission to assist professional linguists. Or you can distribute Bibles where you live. Don't assume everyone in your neighborhood already has the Word of God.

Seek the Lord to know what part you are to play. Invite your church to get involved, but don't be discouraged if they aren't interested. Be open to working with other parts of the body of Christ, and get the blessing of the "gatekeepers."

Ask the Lord who is to be on your team. Meet together and plan what you will commit to, how to share what you're doing with the community, how to raise money for the Bibles, and where you will buy them, whether from a publisher or from one of the Bible societies.

If you are a businessperson, a police chief, a schoolteacher, an IT worker, or any other professional, ask the Holy Spirit how you can be involved. In Youth With A Mission we have partnerships with people in all of the seven spheres. We help mobilize and encourage such groups. We seek even more partnerships with people on the job, showing how they can help end Bible poverty within their workplace or use their professional expertise to contribute to the project elsewhere.

Share this book with others and pray that they will also get involved in ending Bible poverty. Neither my sister Janice

Rogers nor I are taking royalties for this book. We want more funds to go into sharing God's Word with the lost.

Live the Adventure

Going to the uttermost parts of the world is another option. Live the adventure of a lifetime. Come with us to climb the Himalayas, caravan through Central Africa, knock on doors in urban centers, or board a small ship bound for some of the remotest islands on earth.

You can even earn an AA degree from YWAM's University of the Nations while helping to end Bible poverty. For details, see "A Special Opportunity" in the back of this book.

Enough for China, India, and the World

This is the time to take action. Because of the technology God has given us, 80 percent of the world's population has access to the New Testament in the language of their heart. There has never been such preparation for spreading God's Word. We've mentioned the many IT innovations that are ready. Soon satellites will beam down Scripture to handhelds and smartphones, even to those living in countries that are violently opposed to God and his Word.

Don't forget Bibles in print, either. Did you know China is producing the greatest number of Bibles in the world? As we saw in chapter eleven, one group of printers in China alone can crank out one complete Chinese Bible every four seconds. That's fifteen per minute, 900 per hour, 21,600 per day, 129,600 per six-day week, or 6,739,200 per year. They can print 30,326,400 Bibles by Christmas of 2020. And that's still a shortfall for the 47 million homes of China.[1] But if you take into consideration the millions and millions of Chinese homes with internet, we can reach the goal. We can offer God's Word to every home in China, in India, in the world.

What about the ones who are illiterate or who can only read poorly? For these 771 million there are audio Bibles. UniSkript will also allow them to read in their language in two weeks or less.

An Objective and a Deadline

God has released all of these things to make it easier for us to do his will. How can we delay taking God's Word to everyone? It's our responsibility to sow the seed for the mightiest spiritual awakening in history.

Here's a goal for all of us in the body of Christ. A goal has to have a clear, measurable objective, as well as a deadline. Presently there are about 1,776 Bible-less languages, without a single portion of the Bible. Our objective is to offer verbal New Testaments plus the first twelve chapters of Genesis and the *Jesus* film to every household on earth, in their mother tongue. In the second phase of ending Bible poverty we can give them the rest of the Bible.

Our objective also includes offering these to nomadic tribes, the homeless, and those in prisons and institutions. We want to go from 1,776 languages without any portion of the Bible to zero—not one language without a sizable portion of the Bible. Our deadline will be December 25, 2020.[2]

We also want to reach those who have the Bible in their language but don't know about it yet. They've never heard of Jesus, never met a Christian, and have never seen God's book. Our goal is to also offer Bibles to those who don't have one in their home. This is what it means to end Bible poverty now.

December 25, 2020. Can you think of a better birthday gift for Jesus than taking his Word to every home on earth?

Jesus is crying out to you, "Do it!" He's not suggesting it. He's commanding it. Go and disciple all nations. Get his Word out to them. Immerse them in it by teaching them to obey everything he has commanded. Because he has promised, "I am with you always, to the very end of the age" (Matt. 28:19–20).

We can do this. God is going to back us up. He says he's looking all over the world for those who are fully committed to him. What's more, he promises to strengthen us (2 Chron. 16:9). Let's get the Bible into every language. Let's get it onto the internet in more ways. Let's get it out in printed copies. God wants us to be transformed. Then he wants to use us to transform the nations. Because Jesus promised . . .

"Heaven and earth will pass away, but my words will never pass away" (Matt. 24:35).

To become a part of ending Bible poverty,
contact Dax Fears at Kona Bible Office:
Konabibleteam@gmail.com

Appendix A:
A Special Opportunity

Our goal is to take Scripture to each of the 1,776 language groups that have no portion of God's Word. This is my call to you. Join in and receive training while you help end Bible poverty.

You can immerse yourself in the Word of God and participate in field assignments that spread God's Word, all while earning an AA degree with YWAM's University of the Nations.[1]

Attending a Discipleship Training School comes first, in one of our locations in 160 countries. After that you can attend any of our second-level Bible courses. These are numerous and include the ones I mentioned in this book—Word by Heart and School of Biblical Studies. Go to UofN.edu and select "Christian Ministries" for more information on these and more.

In addition, you can choose from different tracks, such as schools for teaching UniSkript or learning from professional Bible translators. Another track would prepare you to assist with film soundtracks or verbal recordings in other languages. As with all University of the Nations courses, your staff will be joined by visiting teachers coming from active work in their special fields. In this AA degree program, many trainers will come from other mission organizations working to end Bible poverty.

Every course is followed by field assignments where you will help professional translators, filmmakers, and audio engineers get God's Word out. Or you may have the thrill of helping a tribe learn to read their own language.

Your field assignments will probably be in various parts of the world. Each school prays and asks the Lord where their teams should go.

All of your training will be aimed at the goal—getting the *Jesus* film and the New Testament plus twelve chapters of Genesis into all of the 1,776 Bible-less languages by Christmas of 2020. Our aim is to go from 1,776 to zero. No one will be able to find a single language without some part of the Word of God. Instead, the Bible will be in all seven thousand languages on earth.

Come, get involved. Be a world changer.

For more information on
the End Bible Poverty Now AA degree,
send an email to Konabibleteam@gmail.com.

Appendix B:
Covenant to End Bible Poverty Now

The goal is one million praying and obeying. Will you also be a multiplier, as Jesus said?

". . . someone who hears the word and understands it. This is the one who produces a crop, yielding a hundred, sixty or thirty times what was sown." (Matt. 13:23)

"Be fruitful and increase in number; fill the earth." (Gen. 1:28)

I commit to the Lord to help end Bible poverty now by praying regularly and doing what the Holy Spirit leads me to do.

Signature: _____

Name: _____

Your nation: _____

With God's help I will mobilize others to go to the website EndBiblePovertyNow.com to sign and commit to pray regularly and obey the Holy Spirit.

___ Just pray ___ 100 others ___ 60 others ___ 30 others

Signature: _____

If you want to be one of the one million signers on a list displayed in public areas such as museums, go to EndBiblePoverty Now.com and sign online. Offer this option to those you mobilize to sign and pray.

Appendix C:
Resources

Books by Loren Cunningham

The Book That Transforms Nations: The Power of the Bible to Change Any Country
Daring to Live on the Edge: The Adventure of Faith and Finances
Is That Really You, God? Hearing the Voice of God
Making Jesus Lord: The Dynamic Power of Laying Down Your Rights
Why Not Women? A Fresh Look at Scripture on Women in Missions, Ministry, and Leadership, with David Hamilton

Other Recommended Books

Vishal Mangalwadi, *The Book that Made Your World: How the Bible Created the Soul of Western Civilization*
Darrow L. Miller with Stan Guthrie, *Discipling Nations: The Power of Truth to Transform Cultures*, 2nd ed.

SourceView and SphereView Bibles

Demo site for SourceView and SphereView:
http://beta.scripturesys.com/
SourceView Suite of Bibles—SourceView, SphereView, and (coming soon) CommandView and VerbView:
https://vimeo.com/138527890
Brief tutorial on SourceView: https://vimeo.com/24106610

Videos

All videos below are available at EndBiblePovertyNow.com; select "Video."
"How to Do an Oral Translation"
"How Bible Translation Works"
"How Bible Translation Works, Part 2"
"Our Lives Tell a Story"
"Your Prayers Help People Get the Bible" (by Wycliffe)

Partner Organizations

American Bible Society: www.americanbible.org
Every Tribe, Every Nation: www.everytribeeverynation.org
Faith Comes By Hearing: www.faithcomesbyhearing.com
Global Recordings: http://globalrecordings.net/en/
International Mission Board: www.imb.org
Issachar Initiative: http://issacharinitiative.org
Jesus Film Project: www.jesusfilm.org
One Story: www.onestory.org
Renew Outreach: www.renewoutreach.com
Pacific Wa'a: http://pacificwaa.org
Pioneers: www.pioneerbible.org
Seed Company: https://theseedcompany.org
SIL: www.sil.org
Transworld Radio: www.twr.org
Wycliffe: www.wycliffe.org

Appendix D:
The Christian Magna Carta

We affirm the Christian Magna Carta, which describes the following basic rights as implicit in the gospel. Everyone on earth has the right to:

- Hear and understand the gospel of Jesus Christ.
- Have a Bible available in their own language.
- Have a Christian fellowship available nearby, to be able to meet for fellowship regularly each week, and to have biblical teaching and worship with others in the body of Christ.
- Have a Christian education available for their children.
- Have the basic necessities of life: food, water, clothing, shelter, and health care.
- Lead a productive life of fulfillment spiritually, mentally, socially, emotionally, and physically.

We commit ourselves, by God's grace, to fulfill this covenant and to live for his glory.

Notes

Chapter 2: It's God's Idea

1. Statistics from Wycliffe Global Alliance, "Scripture & Language Statistics 2015," accessed June 29, 2016, www.wycliffe.net/statistics.

2. "It is estimated that of the 7.2 billion people alive in the world today, 3.0 billion of them live in unreached people groups with little or no access to the Gospel of Jesus Christ." Global Frontier Missions, "Unreached People Groups," accessed September 19, 2016, http://globalfrontiermissions.org /gfm-101-missions-course/the-unreached-peoples-and-their-role-in-the -great-commission/.

Chapter 3: Why Should We End Bible Poverty?

1. Renew World Outreach, "The Reach Strategy," accessed August 15, 2016, www.renewoutreach.com/the-reach-strategy/.

2. The Cold War started after World War II between the communist Soviet Union and its allies and democratic countries of the West. It was a time of tension and threats of nuclear war that continued until 1989 when the communist regimes suddenly collapsed.

Chapter 4: The Bible and Seismic Changes

1. Vishal Mangalwadi, *The Book That Made Your World: How the Bible Created the Soul of Western Civilization* (Nashville: Thomas Nelson, 2011).

2. Ibid., 222.

3. Evidence for God, "Famous Scientists Who Believed in God," last modified December 8, 2011, www.godandscience.org/apologetics/sciencefaith .html, and Henry M. Morris, "Bible-Believing Scientists of the Past," *Acts & Facts* 11, no. 1 (1982), available from Institute for Creation Research, www .icr.org/article/bible-believing-scientists-past/.

4. Evidence for God, "Famous Scientists."

5. Christine Herman, "Study: 2 Million U.S. Scientists Identify as Evangelical," *Christianity Today*, February 20, 2014, www.christianitytoday.com

/ct/2014/february-web-only/study-2-million-scientists-identify-as
-evangelical.html.

6. *Christianity Today*, "George Frideric Handel," Christian History, accessed
May 30, 2016, www.christianitytoday.com/history/people/musiciansartists
andwriters/george-frideric-handel.html.

7. Ibid.

8. Dr. Art Lindsley, "The Priesthood of All Believers," Institute for
Faith, Work & Economics, October 15, 2013, https://tifwe.org/resource
/the-priesthood-of-all-believers/.

9. Exod. 19:6; Isa. 61:6; 1 Pet. 2:5; Rev. 1:6.

10. I first learned of the goals of secular humanism and its attack on America's Christian foundations from Dr. Francis Schaeffer when he taught at our
school in Switzerland. For a quick overview on the humanist takeover of
the educational system, see John Loeffler, "Paradigms, Preaching and Politics: Worldview Wars," Koinonia House, September 2011, www.khouse.org
/articles/2001/365/. Also see Francis A. Schaeffer, "The Abolition of Truth
and Morality," *The Highway*, accessed August 26, 2016, www.the-highway
.com/articleOct01.html.

11. P. Douglas Small, "Were the Roots of Our Country Based Upon
the Bible?" Freedom House, August 1, 2015, www.freedomhousecog.com
/were-the-roots-of-our-country-based-upon-the-bible/.

12. Ibid.

13. "Civil War Casualties," Civil War Trust, accessed August 23, 2016,
www.civilwar.org/education/civil-war-casualties.html.

14. For more stirring accounts of various countries, see my book *The Book
That Transforms Nations: The Power of the Bible to Change Any Country* (Seattle: YWAM Publishing, 2007).

Chapter 5: We Can Do It

1. The Great Schism in AD 1054 divided the Eastern (Orthodox) church
and Western (Roman Catholic) church.

2. The Great Commission is found in many parts of the Bible, most nota-
bly Matt. 28:19–20, Mark 16:15, and Acts 1:8.

3. Cru was formerly known as Campus Crusade for Christ.

Chapter 6: Technologies to Speed the Word

1. Last names withheld for security reasons.

2. These countries cannot be named for security reasons.

3. See the section "Above the Arctic Circle" in chap. 8.

4. Rolf Winkler and Andy Pasztor, "Elon Musk's Next Mission: Internet Satellites," *Wall Street Journal*, updated November 7, 2014, www.wsj.com /articles/elon-musks-next-mission-internet-satellites-1415390062.

5. To see the Vista, go to www.renewoutreach.com/equipment/.

6. Renew World Outreach, "The LightStream," accessed October 10, 2016, www.renewoutreach.com/lightstreams/.

Chapter 7: The Greatest Spread of the Bible in History

1. Sean Coughlan, "Asia Tops Biggest Global School Rankings," BBC News, May 13, 2015, www.bbc.com/news/business-32608772.

2. Bob Eschliman, "Liberty Counsel: School Violated Christian Student's Religious Freedom," *Charisma News*, June 3, 2016, www.charismanews .com/politics/issues/57607-liberty-counsel-school-violated-christian-student-s-religious-freedom.

3. Gary Bates and Lita Cosner, "Pew Survey Reveals Basic Ignorance of Christian Belief," Creation Ministries International, November 2, 2010, http://creation.com/religion-survey-reveals-ignorance-of-bible.

4. From correspondence with Runar Byberg, YWAM Norway.

5. Geoff Waugh, "Revival Fire," accessed August 13, 2016, www.evanwiggs .com/revival/history/revfire.html.

6. Pray for Scotland, "Smith Wigglesworth's 1947 Prophetic Word," accessed June 14, 2016, www.prayforscotland.org.uk/smith-wigglesworths -1947-prophetic-word/.

Chapter 8: How to End Bible Poverty

1. See appendix B for how to sign commitment card online.

2. The Bible Poverty Index (BPI) was created by 4K Mapping in August 2016 to help determine where on the Bible Poverty spectrum a language is located. The full list of languages and their BPI status is the combination of six different organizations' language data (International Mission Board, Jesus Film, Joshua Project, Ethnologue/SIL, Finishing the Task, and eBible), with more to be added in future updates. As you view the list and/or the map, you will see that each language has been placed in one of five categories: No Bible, Translation, Publication, Distribution, and Engagement. By looking at world languages this way, any person with a desire to end Bible poverty can see where they are most needed and called to. The list of every language in the world can be found at endbiblepoverty.org or 4kworldmap. com under the "BPI Data" section of those websites.

3. The Iron Curtain was a metaphor for the political dividing line between the free or Western world and the Communist nations.

4. The *Jesus* film is from the Gospel of Luke. It has been shown over 6 billion times. It is now in 1,400-plus languages, and it needs to be in all 7,000 languages, so YWAM teams are adding this task to their efforts.

Chapter 9: God's Word in Their Heart Language

1. Betty Fullard-Leo, "Henry Opukaha'ia: The Youth Who Changed Hawai'i," *Coffee Times*, accessed June 30, 2016, www.coffeetimes.com /henry.htm.

2. Mokuaikaua Church, "Kailua Kona, Hawai'i's Christian History," accessed September 5, 2016, http://mokuaikaua.com/konahistory/.

3. Gospel Truth Ministries, "Titus Coan: God's Servant," accessed June 30, 2016, www.gospeltruth.net/hawaii_revival.htm.

4. Ibid.

5. Ibid.

6. Titus Coan, *Life in Hawai'i: An Autobiographical Sketch of Mission Life and Labors, 1835–1881* (New York: A. D. F. Randolph, 1882), 154–58.

7. For much more on this topic, see my book *The Book That Transforms Nations: The Power of the Bible to Change Any Country* (Seattle: YWAM Publishing, 2007).

Chapter 10: The Clock Is Racing

1. "SIL Pacific Language Data 2015 Report," conference paper, 2015.

2. Statistics from UNESCO, "Literacy Data Release 2016," accessed August 15, 2016, www.unesco.org.

3. For a brief video demonstrating how local-to-local interpreters work, see "CFZ Curriculum - Oral Learning Motion Graphic," posted by The Issachar Initiative, February 28, 2014, https://vimeo.com/87866960.

4. Sarah Eekhoff Zylstra, "The Unwritten Word of God: Bible Translation Goes Mouth to Mouth," *Christianity Today*, April 24, 2016, www.christianity today.com/ct/2016/may/unwritten-word-god-bible-translation-oral -render-software.html.

Chapter 11: Getting the Word Out

1. The story of how God used the nonbelieving King Cyrus of Persia is told in 2 Chron. 36:22–23; Ezra 1; Isa. 44:24–45:8.

Chapter 12: Spreading Seeds

1. This section is based on Loren Cunningham, *The Book That Transforms Nations: The Power of the Bible to Change Any Country* (Seattle: YWAM Publishing, 2007), 65–71.

2. Trevor Saxby, "The Revival-Bringer: One Man's Initiative Regenerated Norway," *Making History Now* (blog), July 8, 2015, https://making historynow.wordpress.com/2015/07/08/the-country-boy-who-fathered -a-nation-part-1/.

3. Hauge Institute, "About Hans Nielsen Hauge," accessed August 16, 2016, http://haugeinstitute.org/119/about-hans-nielsen-hauge.

4. "Hans Nielsen Hauge," *Wikipedia*, accessed July 7, 2016, https:// en.wikipedia.org/wiki/Hans_Nielsen_Hauge.

5. Ibid.

Chapter 13: Ships, Partner Ships, and a Big Canoe

1. These statistics are current as of 2016, according to the 4K Mapping Project, University of the Nations, Kona, Hawai'i.

Chapter 14: The Gift of Understanding

1. Barna, "The Bible in America: 6-Year Trends," June 15, 2016, www .barna.com/research/the-bible-in-america-6-year-trends/.

2. Abraham Kuyper, a Dutch pastor and prime minister, had a similar set of beliefs regarding three spheres of sovereignty. He divided his three spheres into categories that coincide with those given to me and Bill Bright separately during the summer of 1975. See "Christian Politics According to Abraham Kuyper," accessed August 23, 2016, www.understandingworld religions.com/chapter-summaries/cp_22_summary.pdf.

Chapter 15: Training Outside the Box

1. For more information on the University of the Nations, go to www .uofnkona.edu.

2. Gordon R. Lewis, "Alpha Course: Evaluating Alpha," Christian Research Institute, www.equip.org/article/alpha-course-evaluating-alpha/.

3. Ibid.

4. UniSkript Research & Literacy Institute, "What Is Uniskript?," accessed July 14, 2016, http://uniskript.org/what-is-uniskript. For other information, see YWAM Kona, "Uniskript," accessed August 24, 2016, www.uofn kona.edu/ministries/uniskript/.

5. Merriam-Webster, s.v. "orthography," www.merriam-webster.com /dictionary/orthography.

6. UniSkript Research & Literacy Institute, "What Is Uniskript?"

Chapter 16: Engaging with the Word

1. John Ashcroft, "Worship Heritage and the Modern Church" (video), Evangel University, February 12, 2013, www.evangel.edu/videos/guest-lecture-series-john-ashcroft/. Quote at 4:00.

2. SourceView was developed by David Hamilton. For more information, go to http://sourceviewbible.com/.

Chapter 17: A Dangerous Book

1. Chris Hawley, "11 Mexican Mayors Murdered This Year," *AZ Central*, October 8, 2010, http://archive.azcentral.com/news/articles/2010/10/08/20101008mayors-killed-in-mexico-2010.html.

2. Nick Valencia, "After Years of Violence and Death, 'Life Is Back' in Juarez," *CNN*, April 21, 2015, www.cnn.com/2015/04/21/americas/mexico-ciudad-juarez-tourism/.

3. "Pope Francis to Youth: The Bible Can Change Your Life. Now Read It!," *Catholic News Agency*, October 23, 2015, www.catholicnews agency.com/news/pope-francis-to-youth-the-bible-can-change-your-life-now-read-it-18483/.

Chapter 18: It's Not a Suggestion

1. Some may wonder how over 1.3 billion people can have only 47 million homes. Remember that millions of Chinese households average five people, with three or four generations living together.

2. This number is my computation drawing on those from the Bible translation ministries. They all differ from each other, but the reason is simple. The numbers are changing so fast. The number of Bible-less languages goes down as they complete translations. The number goes up if they discover another language group.

Appendix A: A Special Opportunity

1. University of the Nations is accredited with the Global Accreditation Association of Lausanne, Switzerland for Christian educational institutions from preschool through universities worldwide.